Handbook of
Leftist Guerrilla Groups in
Latin America and the Caribbean

Handbook of Leftist Guerrilla Groups in Latin America and the Caribbean

Liza Gross

in collaboration with the
Council on Hemispheric Affairs

Westview Press

BOULDER • SAN FRANCISCO • OXFORD

Copyright © 1995 by Westview Press, Inc.

Published in 1995 in the United States of America by Westview Press, Inc., 5500 Central Avenue, Boulder, Colorado 80301-2877, and in the United Kingdom by Westview Press, 12 Hid's Copse Road, Cumnor Hill, Oxford OX2 9JJ

Library of Congress Cataloging-in-Publication Data
Gross, Liza.
  Handbook of leftist guerrilla groups in Latin America and the
Caribbean / Liza Gross.
    p. cm.
  Includes bibliographical references.
  ISBN 0-8133-8494-X
  1. Guerrillas—Latin America—History. 2. Guerrillas—Caribbean
Area—History. 3. Latin America—Handbooks, manuals, etc.
4. Caribbean Area—Handbooks, manuals, etc. I. Title.
F1410.G83   1995
972.9—dc20   95-2109
                                                                 CIP

Printed and bound in the United States of America

      The paper used in this publication meets the requirements
      of the American National Standard for Permanence of Paper
      for Printed Library Materials Z39.48-1984.

10   9   8   7   6   5   4   3   2   1

To my son, Martin, and my niece, Clara.
In my eyes, the first one symbolizes
the hope for the future of the generations who left,
and the other the hope for the future
of the generations who stayed.

Contents

Photographs

Acknowledgments

The following interns at the Council on Hemispheric Affairs contributed research and drafts for many of the entries: Heidi Brooks, Beth Chance-Weigel, Matthew Colangelo, Erica DePiero, Elza Hisel, Wyatt Hogan, Greg Hutton, Carlos Lozada, Darin Maney, Brian Nelson, Steve Nish, Melissa Roddy, Brian Sorkin, and David Stern.

The entry on the Montoneros was contributed by Caroline Udall, book editor and former reporter for the defunct English-language biweekly *Times of the Americas*.

I would like to extend special thanks to the following persons for their expert insights and help: Crescencio Arcos, former U.S. ambassador to Honduras and outspoken observer of the reality of that nation; Mario Armando Castro, managing editor of the Guatemalan newspaper *Prensa Libre* and astute interpreter of his country's recent history; Dr. Jorge Domínguez of Harvard University, widely recognized as one of the foremost U.S. authorities on contemporary Cuba; Carlos and Bonnie Grau Dieckmann of Argentina, politically active attorneys and history buffs; Iduvina Hernández, a journalist with a passionate love for her land, whose fascinating tales illuminate Guatemala's many complexities; Gustavo Hiroles, one of the twelve founding members of the Liga Comunista 23 de Septiembre of Mexico and by his own reckoning one of only three who remain alive; distinguished Ecuadoran journalist Edgar Jaramillo of the Centro Internacional de Estudios Superiores de la Comunicación para América Latine (CIESPAL, International Center of Higher Studies of Communication for Latin America); Professor Lou Perez of Florida International University for his explanations concerning Fidel Castro's ideological evolution; Colombian journalist Gerardo Reyes, former member of the investigative unit of the prestigious Bogotá paper *El Tiempo*; Dr. Selwyn Ryan of the University of Trinidad and Tobago for his clarifications regarding Caribbean subversive groups; Jeanneth Sosa of Ecuador, former militant in the ranks of ¡Alfaro Vive, Carajo!; and Eduardo Ulibarri, editor of *La Nación* in San José, Costa Rica, and author of several books on journalism and the role of the journalist in today's society. Intrinsic to any merits possessed by this book is the invaluable research guidance provided to his young scholars by long-time director of the Council on Hemispheric Affairs, Larry Birns.

In addition, the following experts generously gave of their time to review various portions of the book (the specific chapters evaluated appear in parentheses after their names and affiliation): John Booth of the University of North Texas (Costa Rica), Eduardo Gamarra of Florida International University (Bolivia), Donald C. Hodges of Florida State University (Argentina), Cynthia McClintock of George Washington University (Peru), Héctor Santos of the Inter American Development Bank (Dominican Republic), Martin Weinstein of William Paterson College (Uruguay), and Andrew Zimbalist of Smith College (Chile).

I would also like to express my gratitude to Barbara Ellington, my editor at Westview Press, for her patience and cooperative spirit.

Finally, my friend and technodink Duane Dinehart, who helped to preserve my sanity by rescuing my almost completed manuscript from the arcane maze of computer software, deserves my loving appreciation.

Liza Gross

Acronyms

AAA	Alianza Anticomunista Argentina (Argentine Anti-Communist Alliance)
AD	Acción Democrática (Democratic Action, Venezuela)
ALN	Açao Libertadora Nacional (National Liberating Action, Brazil)
ANAPO	Alianza Nacional Popular (Popular National Alliance, Colombia)
APRA	Alianza Popular Revolucionaria Americana (Popular Revolutionary American Alliance, Peru)
ARENA	Alianza Republicana Nacionalista (Nationalist Republican Alliance, El Salvador)
AVC	¡Alfaro Vive, Carajo! (Alfaro Lives, Damn It! Ecuador)
BPR	Bloque Popular Revolucionario (Popular Revolutionary Bloc, El Salvador)
CISPES	Committee in Solidarity with the People of El Salvador
CUC	Comité de Unidad Campesina (Committee of Peasant Unity, Guatemala)
DNU-MRH	Directorio Nacional Unido—Movimientos Revolucionarios Hondureños (United National Directorate—Honduran Revolutionary Movements)
DR	Directorio Revolucionario (Revolutionary Directorate, Cuba)
DRU	Directorio Revolucionario Unificado (Unified Revolutionary Directorate, El Salvador)
EGP	Ejército Guerrillero de los Pobres (Guerrilla Army of the Poor, Guatemala)

EGP	Ejército Guerrillero del Pueblo (Guerrilla Army of the People, Argentina)
ELN	Ejército de Liberación Nacional (Army of National Liberation, Argentina)
ELN	Ejército de Liberación Nacional (Army of National Liberation, Bolivia)
ELN	Ejército de Liberación Nacional (Army of National Liberation, Colombia)
ELN	Ejército de Liberación Nacional (Army of National Liberation, Peru)
EPL	Ejército Popular de Liberación (Popular Army of Liberation, Colombia)
ERP	Ejército Revolucionario del Pueblo (People's Revolutionary Army, Argentina)
ERP	Ejército Revolucionario del Pueblo (People's Revolutionary Army, El Salvador)
EZLN	Ejército Zapatista de Liberación Nacional (Zapatista Army of National Liberation, Mexico)
FAL	Fuerzas Armadas de Liberación (Armed Forces of Liberation, Argentina)
FAL	Fuerzas Armadas de Liberación (Armed Forces of Liberation, El Salvador)
FAP	Fuerzas Armadas Peronistas (Peronist Armed Forces, Argentina)
FAPU	Frente de Acción Popular Unido (United Front of Popular Action, El Salvador)
FAR	Fuerzas Armadas Rebeldes (Rebel Armed Forces, Guatemala)
FAR	Fuerzas Armadas Revolucionarias (Revolutionary Armed Forces, Argentina)
FARC	Fuerzas Armadas Revolucionarias de Colombia (Revolutionary Armed Forces of Colombia)
FARN	Fuerzas Armadas de Resistencia Nacional (Armed Forces of National Resistance, El Salvador)
FARO	Fuerzas Armadas Revolucionarias Orientales (Oriental Revolutionary Armed Forces, Uruguay)
FDR	Frente Democrático Revolucionario (Revolutionary Democratic Front, El Salvador)

FER	Frente Estudiantil Revolucionario (Student Revolutionary Front, Nicaragua)
FIR	Frente Izquierdista Revolucionario (Revolutionary Leftist Front, Peru)
FLN	Frente de Liberación Nacional (National Liberation Front, Venezuela)
FMLN	Frente Farabundo Martí de Liberación Nacional (Farabundo Martí National Liberation Front, El Salvador)
FMLNH	Frente Morazanista de Liberación Nacional Hondureña (Morazanist Front of Honduran National Liberation)
FP-31	Frente Popular 31 de Enero (Popular Front January 31st, Guatemala)
FPL	Fuerzas Populares de Liberación—Farabundo Martí (Popular Forces of Liberation—Farabundo Martí, El Salvador)
FPMR/PCC	Frente Patriótico Manuel Rodríguez/Partido Comunista de Chile (Manuel Rodríguez Patriotic Front/Communist Party of Chile)
FPN	Frente Patriótico Nacional (National Patriotic Front, Nicaragua)
FPR-LZ	Fuerzas Populares Revolucionarias Lorenzo Zelaya (Popular Revolutionary Forces Lorenzo Zelaya, Honduras)
FR	Frente Revolucionario (Revolutionary Front, Peru)
FSLN	Frente Sandinista de Liberación Nacional (Sandinista National Liberation Front, Nicaragua)
FULNA	Frente Unido de Liberación Nacional (United Front of National Liberation, Paraguay)
FUUD	Frente Unido Universitario Democrático (Democratic United University Front, Honduras)
GPP	Guerra Popular Prolongada (Prolonged Popular War)
JEWEL	Joint Endeavor for Welfare, Education and Liberation (Grenada)
JUP	Juventud Uruguaya de Pie (Uruguayan Youth at Attention)

L-23	Liga Comunista 23 de Septiembre (Communist League September 23rd, Mexico)
M-14	Movimiento 14 de Junio (June 14th Movement, Dominican Republic)
M-15	Movimiento 15 de Mayo (May 15th Movement, Peru)
M-19	Movimiento 19 de Abril (April 19th Movement, Colombia)
M-26	Movimiento 26 de Julio (July 26th Movement, Cuba)
MAP	Movement for Assemblies of the People (Grenada)
MIC	Movimiento de Izquierda Cristiana (Christian Left Movement, Ecuador)
MIR	Movimiento de Izquierda Revolucionaria (Movement of the Revolutionary Left, Chile)
MIR	Movimiento de Izquierda Revolucionaria (Movement of the Revolutionary Left, Ecuador)
MIR	Movimiento de Izquierda Revolucionaria (Movement of the Revolutionary Left, Peru)
MIR-FALN	Movimiento de Izquierda Revolucionaria/Fuerzas Armadas de Liberación Nacional (Movement of the Revolutionary Left/Armed Forces of National Liberation, Venezuela)
MLP	Movimiento de Liberación Popular (Movement of Popular Liberation, El Salvador)
MOEC	Movimiento de Obreros, Estudiantes y Campesinos (Movement of Workers, Students and Peasants, Colombia)
MOTC	Movimiento Obreros, Trabajadores y Campesinos (Movement of Workers, Working People and Peasants, Peru)
MPL-Cinchoneros	Movimiento Popular de Liberación "Cinchoneros" (Popular Movement of Liberation "Cinchoneros," Honduras)
MPU	Movimiento del Pueblo Unido (Movement of the United People, Nicaragua)
MR-8	Movimento Revolucionario de Outubre 8 (October 8th Revolutionary Movement, Brazil)

MR-13	Movimiento Revolucionario 13 de Noviembre (Revolutionary Movement November 13th, Guatemala)
MRT	Movimiento Revolucionario de los Trabajadores (Revolutionary Workers' Movement, Ecuador)
MRTA	Movimiento Revolucionario Tupac Amaru (Tupac Amaru Revolutionary Movement, Peru)
NDN	Núcleo de Dirección Nacional (Nucleus of National Leadership, Guatemala)
NJM	New Jewel Movement (Grenada)
OPR-33	Organización Popular Revolucionaria–33 (Popular Revolutionary Organization–33, Uruguay)
OPS	Organización Patriótica Santamaría/Ejército de la Democracia y la Soberanía (Santamaría Patriotic Organization/Army of Democracy and Sovereignty, Costa Rica)
ORDEN	Organización Democrática Nacionalista (Nationalist Democratic Organization, El Salvador)
OREL	Organisation for Research, Education and Liberation (Grenada)
ORPA	Organización Revolucionaria del Pueblo en Armas (Revolutionary Organization of the People in Arms)
PCB	Partido Comunista Boliviano (Bolivian Communist Party)
PCB	Partido Comunista Brasileiro (Brazilian Communist Party)
PCC	Partido Comunista de Chile (Communist Party of Chile)
PCC-ML	Partido Comunista Colombiano—Marxista Leninista (Colombian Communist Party—Marxist-Leninist)
PCES	Partido Comunista de El Salvador (Communist Party of El Salvador)
PCH	Partido Comunista de Honduras (Communist Party of Honduras)
PCP	Partido Comunista Peruano (Peruvian Communist Party)

PCP-BR   Partido Comunista del Perú—Bandera Roja
                (Communist Party of Peru—Red Flag)
PCV-FALN   Partido Comunista de Venezuela/Fuerzas
                Armadas de Liberación Nacional (Communist
                Party of Venezuela/Armed Forces of National
                Liberation, Venezuela)
PDC   Partido Demócrata Cristiano (Christian Democratic
                Party, El Salvador)
PGT-FAR   Partido Guatemalteco del Trabajo/Fuerzas
                Armadas Revolucionarias (Guatemalan Labor
                Party/Revolutionary Armed Forces)
POR   Partido Obrero Revolucionario (Revolutionary
                Workers' Party, Peru)
PRA   People's Revolutionary Army (Grenada)
PRI   Partido Revolucionario Institucional (Institutional
                Revolutionary Party, Mexico)
PRN   Partido de Resistencia Nacional (National
                Resistance Party, El Salvador)
PROCUP/PdlP   Partido Revolucionario de Obreros y Campesinos/
                Partido de los Pobres (Revolutionary Party of
                Workers and Peasants/Party of the Poor,
                Mexico)
PRTC   Partido Revolucionario de Trabajadores de
                Centroamérica (Revolutionary Party of the
                Workers of Central America, El Salvador)
PRTC/FALP   Partido Revolucionario de Trabajadores de
                Centroamérica/Fuerzas Armadas
                Revolucionarias de Liberación Popular
                (Revolutionary Party of the Workers of Central
                America/Armed Revolutionary Forces of
                Popular Liberation, El Salvador)
PRTCH   Partido Revolucionario de Trabajadores
                Centroamericanos—Honduras (Revolutionary
                Party of Central American Workers—Honduras)
PSP   Partido Socialista Popular (Socialist Popular Party,
                Cuba)
PST   Partido Socialista de los Trabajadores (Socialist
                Workers' Party, Chile)

RN	Resistencia Nacional (National Resistance, El Salvador)
TP	Tendencia Proletaria (Proletarian Tendency, Nicaragua)
UDN	Unión Democrática Nacionalista (Nationalist Democratic Union)
UNO	Unión Nacional Opositora (National Union of Opposition)
UP	Unidad Patriótica (Patriotic Unity, Colombia)
URNG	Unidad Revolucionaria Nacional Guatemalteca (Guatemalan National Revolutionary Unit)
VPR	Vanguardia Popular Revolucionaria (Popular Revolutionary Vanguard, Brazil)

INTRODUCTION

Although united by common language roots (Portuguese, like Spanish, is a Romance language) and a staunch Catholic tradition, Latin American countries present significant geographical, social, and economic variations. In terms of size, El Salvador is the equivalent of a medium-sized Argentine province. The geophysical makeup of Peru, with its impenetrable jungles and forbidding mountains, offers a marked contrast to the idyllic tropical landscape of Cuba. The ethnic composition of Uruguay diverges greatly from that of Guatemala, with its heavy indigenous component. Levels of literacy in Chile are much higher than those in Nicaragua. Mexico City is considered the largest city in the world, but Tegucigalpa's downtown area barely exceeds a few square blocks.

The unique characteristics of each Latin American nation, the circumstances and conditions that set it apart from its neighbors, are just too numerous to record. Yet, in virtually all of these countries, one single phenomenon has flourished unabated from the late 1950s until today: leftist guerrilla activity. Its goal: taking power and installing a new social and political order.

In the second half of the twentieth century, a new, imported ideology hit the Americas. Marxism-Leninism and its related theories—Trotskyism, Maoism, Guevarism, Castrism—mixed with nationalist ideologies to spark revolutionary upheaval. The triumph of the Cuban guerrilla fighters in 1959 gave impetus to a fire that spread along mountains, jungles, rural areas, and cities in Mexico, Central America, and South America.

Except for Fidel Castro in Cuba, the Sandinistas in Nicaragua, and the New Jewel Movement in Grenada, cases that constitute the exception rather than the rule, these revolutionaries never accomplished their aim of taking power and installing a new social and political order along Communist lines. In most instances, though, they made a deep impression well out of proportion with the numbers of their followers or the strength of their financial and logistical resources. Although it is virtually impossible to offer a precise figure, the combined strength of leftist guerrilla forces in the hemisphere over their entire history to date of some forty years has never exceeded 50,000. Yet these groups have affected the lives of millions and on several occasions have even dictated the hemispheric foreign policy of the United States. Indeed, their impact has been so enduring that some societies, like those of Argentina and Nicaragua, remain sharply divided along battle lines drawn at the heyday of leftist guerrilla activity.

Despite their prominent role in the contemporary history of Latin America, leftist guerrilla movements remain a challenging topic of scholarly study. A given group typically receives only cursory treatment within the parameters of a larger study or in news items devoid of contextual reference. Propagandistic literature portrays guerrillas as caricaturesque heroes or villains, depending on the author's point of view. Also, by their very nature, leftist guerrilla groups are secretive. Consequently, information is not plentiful or easy to verify. The existing works devoted exclusively to leftist guerrilla groups, most excellent in depth, are outdated or consider only one individual movement or just a few of them.

In addition, gathered data about the leftist guerrilla phenomenon are open to misinterpretation. It often becomes the object of pseudophilosophical debate in which the prevailing ideological position tends to mix, confuse, or accommodate the issues, frequently at the expense of substance. This attitude can best be illustrated by the comment of an analyst from the Washington Office on Latin America, a nonprofit organization that specializes in the region. When I requested information about important dates related to a certain guerrilla group, this specialist, who prepares reports about the region, replied: "We don't deal in facts here. We deal in analysis."

This handbook represents a modest effort to provide a factual foundation of the subject by systematizing currently available data about leftist guerrilla movements in the hemisphere. These movements encompass only leftist organizations that take up arms and not the legal groups that work for change within the system, right-wing groups, nationalist movements, or those fighting exclusively for minority rights. For this book I used the following selective criteria for identifying leftist guerrilla groups:

1. They are driven by a leftist ideology, whether Marxist-Leninist, Trotskyist, Maoist, Guevarist, or Castrist. Usually this ideology is not pure but mixed with nationalist, populist, and even fascist elements. Still, the leftist aspect animates the overall ideological makeup of the group. The Quintín Lamé of Colombia, for example, was not included because it was mainly interested in giving a voice to the claims of the Indians and used a leftist ideology subordinated to this narrower objective. Also, many groups that start out using a particular ideological banner may end up subscribing to a different theory, and other groups show ideological confusion, mixing concepts indiscriminately or never specifying a clear agenda through communiqués, manifestos, or other documents.

2. They seek the subversion of the established sociopolitical structure and its replacement by a Marxist or Marxism-inspired state. By definition, subversion means to upset a set of values in order to replace them with a new system. Thus, groups like the Macheteros of Puerto Rico and the Mouvement de Liberation Nationale (National Liberation Movement) of Guadeloupe are not considered, since they were and are mainly national movements engaged in the overthrow of a colonial power (the United States and France, respectively), even though their ideologies present definite leftist overtones.

3. They are committed to armed struggle. Subversion does not necessarily imply armed struggle. Many Communist and Socialist parties in the hemisphere, as well as a host of militant groups, have advocated the replacement of the political status quo but have not contemplated armed struggle as a viable means of achieving it.

Leftist guerrilla groups cannot conceive of change without the notion of armed struggle. A revolutionary war that could exacerbate the contradictions in the existing system and spark the uprising of the masses is one of their raisons d'être. In fact, many guerrilla organizations evolve from splinter groups seceding from regional Communist parties that reject the option of armed struggle.

4. The groups are clandestine for their entire existence or part of it. This characteristic shows them up as a threat to the dominant power structure and indicates their inability to survive as open organizations.

This book does not offer analysis or interpretations of contemporary Latin America and the Caribbean. Historical background on each country is only included inasmuch as it relates directly to the guerrilla group considered. The book does not pretend to serve up any spectacular revelations either. Its purpose, as stated previously, is to gather and process existing information in one comprehensive source. Whenever possible, all data, from statistics, dates, and spellings of names to tactical decisions or descriptions of ideology, were confirmed by several sources. I discarded or qualified information that could not be conclusively corroborated. In general, I deemed primary sources more valuable than secondary sources and balanced accounts more reliable than texts written from an extreme political viewpoint. Key sources have been listed in a brief annotated bibliography at the end of each country entry. Additional sources are cited in the bibliography that appears at the end of the book.

Still, the very process of collecting and organizing this material, as well as the wide scope of the approach, inevitably led to some reflections on violence and its role in the region.

One of the keys to understanding the Latin American mind-set is the awareness that, both in its communities and among individuals, there exists a strong tradition of resorting to violent means in order to settle, suppress, or challenge sociopolitical conflict. Even before the arrival of the Europeans in the Americas, pre-Columbian civilizations had their own brand of nonpeaceful behaviors and perpetually engaged in wars and fights among themselves. In the nineteenth century, inspired by the French and American Revolutions, figures like Simón Bolívar and José de San Martín, children of the European Enlightenment, fought a bloody trail to eliminate the Spanish presence from Latin American soil and forge political self-determination for the young republics, many of which promptly engaged in internal disputes once established. The Mexican Revolution, La Violencia in Colombia, and the Argentine Guerra Sucia are some chilling examples of the levels of ferocity that can be reached in Latin America.

In this respect, leftist guerrilla movements did not deviate from the norm. Independent of their rhetoric to explain away the use of violence as part of a sociopolitical strategy, many guerrilla fighters have favored this option because they have been intrinsically violent. I do not mean to suggest that all leftists engaged in armed struggle were using ideologies and ideals as a pretext for violence, but the romantic view of the pure revolutionary fighting for a better world in harmonious agreement with other comrades is quickly shattered by evidence of the internal fighting and bloody purges that have been a constant in many of these groups. In addition, many guerrillas have exhibited questionable psychological motives cloaked as legitimate political agendas. A former Mexican guerrilla interviewed for this work recounted the story of how an Argentine fighter nicknamed El Pibe (The Kid) left Mexico after the defeat of the Liga 23 de Septiembre saying, "There is no action here and I cannot live without blood." And how can the gratuitous atrocities committed by Sendero Luminoso of Peru, such as cutting off the hands of peasants, be understood as an honorable part of armed struggle?

That same former guerrilla jokingly commented that, shortly before the appearance of the Ejército Zapatista de Liberación Nacional (EZLN, Zapatista Army of National Liberation) on January 1, 1994, he had written an article flatly discounting the possibility of a new guerrilla movement appearing in Mexico. Miscalculations aside, even if the EZLN manages to maintain momentum, the group is bucking a historical trend going in the exact opposite direction. Except for the three above-mentioned successes (in Cuba, Nicaragua, and Grenada), a quick assessment indicates that this revolutionary wave of the second half of the twentieth century has been a spectacular practical failure, with leftist guerrilla movements meeting one of four fates: (1) total annihilation at the hands of armed security forces; (2) voluntary dissolution, either through public announcement or gradually without public announcement; (3) transformation into a mainstream political force; and (4) persistence in the armed struggle, even in the face of the realization that the possibility of attaining power is virtually nil. Here the agenda appears to have become one of plain lawless banditry increasingly divorced from any ideological guiding principles.

But to evaluate the phenomenon merely from the standpoint of winners and losers overlooks a much more fundamental issue. Beyond its balance in the historical ledger of successes and failures, leftist guerrilla activity must be seen as the other side of the coin of yet another, much larger, form of violence—the institutionalized violence perpetrated by the existing power structures in the region. Leftist guerrilla movements responded with their own version of violence to the violations inflicted upon the urban and rural disenfranchised at the hands of oppressive and repressive governing oligarchies.

The ambivalent attitudes about the guerrilla legacy is clearly reflected in the recent comments of four Guatemalans. Although they were speaking specifically about the situation in their own country, their wildly disparate opinions and perceptions of the guerrillas' impact could be found just about anywhere on the continent. While I was enjoying the exquisite hospitality of his luxurious home, an anthropologist turned coffee businessman explained to me, "There are three kinds of guerrillas in

Central America: the Nicaraguans, who won; the Salvadorans, who tied; and the Guatemalans, who lost and will have to sign a disadvantageous peace." I repeated this statement to a technocrat who occupies a high management position at a Guatemalan daily and whose family includes members of the military. He flatly disregarded the businessman's statement, saying: "The guerrillas did win. They gave an identity to the Indians. Before the war, they were invisible." Another journalist, a reporter with extensive experience covering the military and the situation of the refugees returning from the Mexican border, agreed with the businessman's statement about the Guatemalan guerrilla but disagreed with respect to the Salvadoran guerrilla. Finally, a graphic artist who in the past had some involvement with peasant education initiatives carried out by the military suggested that the guerrillas are set up to resist for another forty years, regardless of the peace negotiations.

The conditions that brought the leftist guerrilla movements into existence have not changed significantly. Many of Latin America's socioeconomic needs are at least as urgent as they were forty years ago. In fact, in many Latin American countries the disparities between the haves and the have-nots are growing larger by the day.

As thousands of refugees, relatives, and friends of the disappeared and of exiles can attest, violence is a very painful and ultimately unworkable alternative both as a modus operandi and as a modus vivendi. Extremism, whether from the right or from the left, does not provide real, lasting solutions to the problems of hunger, inequality, poverty, and political disempowerment. Almost half a century after the first outbreaks of leftist guerrilla activity in the region and tens of thousands of dead later, the puzzle to meaningful and legitimate structural change in Latin America and the Caribbean remains unsolved.

1

ARGENTINA

EJERCITO GUERRILLERO DEL PUEBLO (EGP)
Guerrilla Army of the People

Active from 1963 to 1964; Marxist-Leninist, Guevarist; operated mainly in the northwestern province of Salta; led by Ricardo Jorge Massetti, Hermes Peña, and Lázaro Peña.

In June 1963, a group led by Peronist Ricardo Jorge Massetti arrived in Bolivia from Cuba and set up a guerrilla training camp near the Argentine border. In September of that year, Massetti filtered men and arms into Argentina and created a *foco* (a small band of guerrillas operating in the rural areas in accordance with a doctrine of guerrilla warfare codified by Ernesto "Che" Guevara and Régis Debray) in the province of Salta in northwestern Argentina. Massetti was a journalist and founder of the Cuban news agency Prensa Latina. His nom de guerre was Comandante Segundo, after Guevara, who was the first.

The organization's goal was to work among peasants, teaching them how to read and write and instructing them about the revolution. When President Arturo Illia of the Partido Radical (Radical Party) was elected in 1963, the EGP denounced the government as anti–grass roots.

The EGP engaged in military action in 1964 by ambushing a border patrol. But without a clear political program and with insufficient military training, the group was easily wiped out by the Argentine border patrol later that year. Massetti fled to the jungle and never reappeared.

EJERCITO REVOLUCIONARIO DEL PUEBLO (ERP)
People's Revolutionary Army

Founded in 1970; operated mainly in the capital city of Buenos Aires, the province of Buenos Aires, and the northwestern province of Tucumán; initially Trotskyist, then Guevarist; led by Mario Roberto Santucho, Enrique Harold Gorriarán Merlo, José Benito Urteaga, Juan Eliseo Ledesma, and Luis Mattini; its most spectacular operation was the "liberation" of Tucumán; obtained funds mostly from kidnapping ransoms.

The Ejército Revolucionario del Pueblo was Argentina's most notorious and effective Communist guerrilla organization from its birth in 1970 to its definitive defeat in 1977. At the peak of its strength, the organization numbered some 550 combatants.

The ERP was born at the Fifth Congress of the Trotskyist Partido Revolucionario de los Trabajadores (Revolutionary Workers' Party), held in a farmhouse near the city of San Nicolás in the province of Buenos Aires in July 1970. The party decided it needed a guerrilla vanguard organization to hasten the advent of socialism. The ERP, under the leadership of Mario Roberto Santucho, was to be the armed force that would overthrow Argentine capitalism and rally the workers to demand the immediate creation of a socialist economy. In its "first military plan," the group contemplated actions such as funds expropriation, occupation of communities, release of prisoners, and kidnappings.

Argentine revolutionary Ernesto "Che" Guevara was the ERP's role model. In an interview with Intercontinental Press on May 28, 1973, two of the ERP's official spokesmen elaborated on Guevara's influence on the ERP's structure and methods of organization: "We recognize Ernesto Che Guevara as the top commander in the revolutionary war on which we have embarked. And this is not a mere ... expression of personal affinity. It also stems from a general agreement with his strategic conceptions for developing the revolution: create two, three, many Vietnams, with one or several of them in Latin America" (Hodges 1974: 112–113).

The ERP had little doctrinal tolerance for the other guerrilla groups in Argentina of Peronist origin, especially the Fuerzas Armadas Revolucionarias (FAR, Revolutionary Armed Forces). The ERP considered Peronism a fundamentally bourgeois movement that only weakened the working class by quelling its revolutionary instincts. According to the revolutionaries, *Peronismo* was antiproletarian because of its wide support among industrialists, the military, and other reactionary elements of society, was too nationalistic, and made the Argentine workers lose perspective of the fact that Marxism-Leninism was a struggle to be carried out on an international basis. Despite these criticisms, the ERP cooperated with Peronist guerrilla groups on various operations. The organization also strongly opposed the Partido Comunista Argentino (Argentine

Communist Party), of Marxist-Leninist orientation, and considered the organization fascist and bureaucratic.

Although active in 1970 and 1971, the ERP did not engage in major initiatives and become known throughout the country until 1972. During that year, the group kidnapped business executives, often foreign nationals, and attacked military bases. In early April, the ERP joined the FAR in the execution of General Juan Carlos Sánchez, commander of the 2nd Army Corps in Córdoba, in retaliation for his role in the suppression of the second *Cordobazo*, a series of protests by workers and students in the provincial capital of Córdoba in March 1971.

On March 21, 1972, the ERP kidnapped Oberdan Sallustro, the head of Fiat-Concord, Fiat Motor Company's Argentine subsidiary, in an effort to get fired workers back on the job and to secure the freedom of fifty imprisoned guerrillas, who would be flown to Algiers. The kidnappers also demanded payment of ransom and distribution of school supplies for destitute children. Despite negotiations, the government forbade the payment of ransom and Sallustro was killed April 10 when the *cárcel del pueblo* (prison of the people) where he was being held was discovered by police.

On August 15, twenty-five militants from the ERP, the FAR, and the Montoneros escaped from the Rawson Penitentiary in Patagonia. They soon surrendered at the Trelew Airport. Although the local Peronist Party begged Interior Minister Arturo Mor Roig not to allow the prisoners to be summarily executed by the military, sixteen of the militants were executed at the Almirante Zar naval base five days later. Among those killed was the wife of ERP founder Santucho. The government abducted three of the bodies, which were being kept at the Peronist Party headquarters, to hide the fact that they had been murdered.

With the imminent return of exiled leader Juan Domingo Perón, who was living in Spain following his overthrow in 1956 by the Argentine military, the ERP suffered internal fragmentation. Although the ERP officially condemned Peronism, a small group of ERP members came out in open support of the Peronist ticket prior to the 1973 national elections. They called themselves the ERP 22 but never attained the status or importance of the mother organization. Another important ideological crisis resulted when the ERP broke ties with the Trotskyist international movement. The organization declared it was trying to "proletarianize" itself, which meant it was going to concentrate more on the unique historical experience and conditions of the Argentine underclass.

The guerrillas' major actions of 1973 began on May 24 with the kidnapping of a Ford Motor Company executive in Buenos Aires. He was released in exchange for $1 million in food and clothing for the dwellers of the city's sprawling slums. On December 6 of that year, ERP insurgents carried out their most lucrative kidnapping effort. Robert Samuelson, the general manager of Exxon Oil, was kidnapped and released for a $14 million ransom.

It was another event, however, that would dramatically alter the group's future—the Perón government's decision to outlaw the ERP in September of 1973. When Perón returned to Argentina to lead the country, there was civil strife between Communists and others on the Left and industrialists and the military on the Right for the soul and backing of the Peronist government. Perón had no patience for the violent methods of groups like the ERP, especially after the ERP harshly criticized the social pact developed by the government to split the national income more equitably between labor and capital. He did not object when the military took steps to organize special units to hunt down and destroy leftist guerrilla cells. These units soon turned into right-wing death squads, which plagued Argentina for years.

The ERP welcomed the harsh response of the armed forces. It believed this reaction fit in well with its plans to topple the civilian government through internal chaos and force the military to take control of the country through severely repressive means. This military repression of society would highlight the contradictions of the ruling system and expose its true repressive nature. This undeniable evidence would then spark a popular revolution to overthrow the corrupt ruling order.

The ERP began the year 1974 with a bold and successful assault on the army barracks in Azul, an act the army and the government considered deeply humiliating. In February, the guerrilla group modified its previous inward focus on Argentina and formed a regional bloc with Communist rebel groups from the Southern Cone, including the Tupamaros from Uruguay, the Movimiento de Izquierda Revolucionaria (MIR, Movement of the Revolutionary Left) from Chile, and the Ejército de Liberación Nacional (ELN, Army of National Liberation) from Bolivia. The command center, the Comité Coordinador Revolucionario (Revolutionary Coordinating Committee), hoped to organize joint actions to be carried out by multinational cells.

In the final months of 1974, the ERP carried out its most audacious attacks, while at the same time the groundwork was laid for its ultimate defeat as government security forces formed units to hunt down the ERP and other leftist groups and their supporters. In October, the ERP assassinated Jordán Genta, an author with deeply anti-Semitic, nationalistic views and a staunch proponent of immediate and total military control of the government. Following Perón's death, the Fuerzas Armadas Peronistas (FAP, Peronist Armed Forces), once a Peronist group, began to cooperate more closely with the ERP.

On October 26, the FAP issued a communiqué accepting Marxism-Leninism and stating the group's subordination into the project of the Partido Revolucionario de los Trabajadores (Revolutionary Workers' Party) and incorporation into the ranks of the ERP. This announcement marked the first time a Peronist armed movement had switched over to Guevarism.

The movement's most famous operation, the "liberation" of Tucumán, took place in November 1974. Tucumán is a destitute, densely populated sugar-growing province in northwestern Argentina. It is also the site of the declaration of Argentine independence from Spain in 1816. The ERP planned to seize the area, educate the inhabitants about their miserable conditions, and eventually develop a socialist economy. It succeeded in recruiting a few villagers, exacting economic tributes, and occupying a few small communities. But the government quickly responded. Isabel Perón, who had become president following her husband's death, signed "Operación Independencia" (Operation Independence), an executive order allowing the armed forces to use whatever means necessary to neutralize the subversive elements in Tucumán. Seven months later, she extended the mandate, which had become a license for mass murder.

A year later, elements of the forces organized the Alianza Anticomunista Argentina (AAA, Argentine Anti-Communist Alliance), which was nothing more than a right-wing death squad to hunt and kill leftist guerrillas and their sympathizers. The AAA formed in direct response to the ERP's pledge to start indiscriminately killing military personnel.

The year 1975 marked the last year the ERP functioned as an organized guerrilla movement. On April 13, it carried out its last successful raid on a military base, this time on the 121st Arsenal in San Lorenzo in the province of Santa Fe. December 23 marked the ERP's Waterloo with its disastrous raid on the military arsenal of Domingo Viejo, south of Buenos Aires. In the fierce battle, the ERP lost nearly 100 of the 200 guerrillas who began the attack. The military sustained only a handful of casualties.

After the failed effort, the organization went into a downward spiral. Money and weapons became scarcer. The government was ruthlessly effective in killing active guerrillas and dismantling their network of support by torturing those captured to elicit the identities of other supporters. The population was weary of violence and the ERP's popular support decreased rapidly. In the organization's last internal bulletin in Argentina, founder Santucho wrote of ceasing guerrilla activities in favor of a purely political struggle.

But he never got the opportunity to carry out this shift in objectives. On July 19, 1976, an army unit burst into an apartment in Villa Martelli, in the province of Buenos Aires, where Santucho and José Benito Urteaga were hiding, along with Santucho's common-law wife, Liliana Delfino, and Urteaga's child. Santucho was shot dead as he tried to escape through a window. Ironically, he was set to leave Argentina for Havana, using a false passport, on that same day. Santucho's death was the final nail in the coffin of the ERP's existence as an effective guerrilla movement.

In 1979 the Partido Revolucionario de los Trabajadores divided into two groups. The first one, headed by Luis Mattini, Amílcar Santucho (Mario Roberto Santucho's brother), and Roberto Guevara (Che's brother), gave up on armed struggle, dissolved the ERP, and began to work toward reentering mainstream politics. The second group, headed by Enrique Harold Gorriarán Merlo and Hugo Irurzún, continued to support armed struggle and left for Nicaragua to collaborate with the Sandinistas. On September 17, 1980, Irurzún and Gorriarán Merlo planned and executed the assassination of former Nicaraguan dictator Anastasio Somoza in Asunción, Paraguay.

On January 24, 1989, Gorriarán Merlo led an unsuccessful attack against the military barracks at La Tablada, in Buenos Aires province. Many of the fighters were former ERP combatants. Gorriarán Merlo managed to escape and is believed to now live in Cuba.

FUERZAS ARMADAS DE LIBERACION (FAL)
Armed Forces of Liberation

Active between 1969 and the mid-1970s in the province of Buenos Aires; Marxist-Leninist with Maoist overtones; led by Eduardo Jozami; fused with the Montoneros and with the Ejército Revolucionario del Pueblo.

The members of the Fuerzas Armadas de Liberación supported the Cuban revolution and national liberation movements and believed in an armed vanguard that would galvanize the people through organized revolutionary violence.

The group began its armed struggle on April 5, 1969, with an attack on the Campo de Mayo army barracks in Buenos Aires. Several FAL actions drew attention in 1970. In March of that year, the group kidnapped the Paraguayan consul in Buenos Aires in order to exchange him for two imprisoned militants. The organization led an attack against a bank in June, and in October, members threw FAL leaflets from a plane they had skyjacked. In November, the FAL assassinated the head of Political Affairs of the Federal Police, Oswaldo Sandoval.

The FAL never managed to attain an important position among armed leftist groups. In 1974, a splinter group of the FAL, the Comandos Populares de Liberación (Popular Commandos of Liberation), headed by Eduardo Jozami, joined the Montoneros. Other factions of the organization allied with the Ejército Revolucionario del Pueblo.

FUERZAS ARMADAS PERONISTAS (FAP)
Peronist Armed Forces

Initiated activity in 1967; operated in Tucumán province and Buenos Aires, both the capital city and the province of the same name; leftist Peronist; led by Envar El Kadri, Carlos Caride, Arturo Gadea, Gerardo Ferrari, and Miguel Zabala Rodríguez; began decline in 1973; members were eventually absorbed into other groups.

The 17 de Octubre detachment of the Fuerzas Armadas Peronistas was established in the beginning of 1967 at an encampment called El Plumerillo, located in Taco Ralo in the province of Tucumán. The group would remain the main ideological force of the Peronist Left until 1972. The purpose of the FAP was to wage urban and rural guerrilla warfare. Its cadres were made up of experienced Peronist militants as well as elements of rightist nationalist groups like Movimiento Nacionalista Revolucionario Tacuara (Tacuara Nationalist Revolutionary Movement). Despite divergent ideologies, members shared an admiration for the Cuban and Algerian experiences and believed in *guerra popular prolongada* (prolonged popular war) and the organization of the masses.

On September 20, 1968, the FAP suffered a very serious defeat when thirteen of its guerrillas were captured in Taco Ralo. Despite this setback and the imprisonment of leader Carlos Caride in April 1969, the group managed to reorganize itself for urban warfare and kept up a series of attacks throughout 1970. The main actions that year included an attack on a housing development for petty officers in Campo de Mayo barracks, an attack in April against the Maritime National Headquarters in Tigre in the province of Buenos Aires, and the theft of 600 boxes of dynamite destined for the El Chocón dam in September.

After 1972, the FAP could not maintain its preeminent position in the Peronist movement because of infighting and the imprisonment of its main leaders. El Kadri and Caride remained in jail until 1973. Following leader Juan Domingo Perón's death in 1974, the FAP began to cooperate more closely with the Ejército Revolucionario del Pueblo. On October 26, the FAP issued a communiqué accepting Marxism-Leninism and incorporating itself into the ranks of the ERP. This event marked the first time a Peronist armed movement had switched over to Guevarism.

Eventually, the various splinter groups of the FAP were absorbed into other guerrilla movements. Caride, for example, joined the Montoneros and was killed in 1976. Zabala Rodríguez became a representative for the Juventud Peronista (Peronist Youth) but eventually had to go underground and was killed on Christmas Day in 1976.

FUERZAS ARMADAS REVOLUCIONARIAS (FAR)
Revolutionary Armed Forces

Operated from 1967 to 1973 in the city of Buenos Aires, Buenos Aires province, and Córdoba province; Marxist-Leninist-Peronist; led by Carlos Enrique Olmedo, Juan Pablo Maestre, Sara Palacios, Mirta Misetich, Marcos Osatinsky, Roberto Quieto, and Marcelo Kurlat; obtained funds through robberies and kidnappings; attempted and failed to unite Argentina's insurgent movements into a common front.

The Fuerzas Armadas Revolucionarias was a small, pro-Cuba organization founded in 1967 by dissidents of the Partido Socialista de Vanguardia (Vanguard Socialist Party) and the Partido Comunista Argentino. In a period now known as the "proto-FAR," these same revolutionaries had founded the Ejército de Liberación Nacional (ELN, Army of National Liberation) with the intention of joining Che Guevara's guerrillas in Bolivia. Che's defeat in Bolivia, however, had forced the militants to rethink their strategy and turn toward urban insurgency with a Peronist ideology.

The FAR orchestrated its actions in order to painstakingly develop its organizational capability. It started out with a "rehearsal" on July 26,

1969, when it bombed thirteen Minimax supermarkets (Rockefeller-owned) shortly before Governor Nelson Rockefeller arrived in Buenos Aires. It did not, however, take public credit for that action.

Its real debut came at the time of the coup against General Juan Carlos Onganía, who had deposed constitutionally elected president Arturo Illia. The guerrillas occupied the town of Garín, in the province of Buenos Aires, already using the name FAR, on July 30, 1970.

After the Garín episode, which had been given the code name Gabriela, the FAR was fairly active for the rest of the year. On October 21 it attacked Córdoba's police station, destroying several vehicles with flame throwers. On November 18, FAR militants robbed a bank in Gerli in the province of Buenos Aires, and on December 15 they robbed the Banco Comercial de la Plata. Two policemen were killed in the latter action. In December, a FAR unit attacked yet another bank. In that month, militant Raquel Liliana Gelin was killed in a shootout with police in Córdoba province.

On March 25, 1971, a FAR commando seized documents from the Office of Vital Statistics in Buenos Aires. On April 4, rebels occupied a police station in Virreyes, Buenos Aires province, seizing weapons and uniforms, and on December 15, 1971, they dynamited a police station outside Buenos Aires.

The capture of four militants in Córdoba in early 1971 and the subsequent seizure of vital data by security forces temporarily halted the FAR's development and directed a return to actions of tactical importance. One of its leaders, Juan Pablo Maestre, was executed on July 15, apparently by death squads.

At around this time, the FAR initiated a program to unite all of Argentina's insurgent movements into a common front, envisioning a program of *ejército del pueblo, guerra del pueblo* (people's army, people's war) (Kohl 1974: 327). Its theorists became convinced that in matters of revolutionary theory, nationalism was the key.

The FAR called itself Marxist-Leninist-Peronist—Marxism-Leninism was the theoretical instrument of social analysis and Peronism the expression of the experience of the Argentine masses. Many FAR leaders received revolutionary training in Cuba, but their initial fighting manual was *Rebellion in the Holy Land*, written by Menachem Begin when his Irgun movement was waging a terrorist campaign against the British prior to the creation of the state of Israel. Initially, FAR militants were mostly Guevarists, as well as dissident elements of the Communist Party, the

Trotskyite movement, and other leftist groups. Later, elements from other armed groups, such as the FAL, joined the FAR.

The Peronist electoral victory in 1973 and its aftermath prompted a reassessment of the situation by urban guerrillas in Argentina. The strategy following the Trelew massacre had addressed itself to revolutionary justice and the approaching presidential elections of March 1973. Revolutionary justice involved reprisals against officers held directly responsible for Trelew and began with the assassination of Admiral Emilio R. Berisso, the ranking naval intelligence officer, on December 28, 1972. A combined ERP-FAR-Montonero commando brigade claimed responsibility for the action, the first in a series of assassinations and kidnappings of military officers.

Most Peronist guerrillas supported Peronist candidate Héctor Cámpora's presidential candidacy with the proviso that revolutionary change follow electoral victory. After exiled leader Juan Domingo Perón's return, the FAR continued to maintain critical support for the Peronist movement, although when President Cámpora demanded that all clandestine organizations give up their weapons after his May 15, 1973, inauguration, the FAR refused. In 1973, the FAR fused with the Montoneros.

MOVIMIENTO PERONISTA MONTONERO (Montoneros)
Montonero Peronist Movement

Active from 1969 to 1977; leftist Peronist faction with initial fascist roots, nationalistic with radical Catholic social agenda; most spectacular operations included the kidnapping and execution of former president Pedro Eugenio Aramburu in 1970 and the kidnapping of industrialists Juan and Jorge Born for $60 million ransom in 1974; led by Fernando Abal Medina, Carlos Gustavo Ramus, and Mario Firmenich; its legal front organization was the Juventud Peronista-Regionales; decimated by counterinsurgency of the military government that ruled from 1976 to 1983.

On May 29, 1970, two young men in military uniform called on Argentina's ex-president Pedro Aramburu in his apartment in Buenos Aires. After telling the retired general, who ruled the country from 1955–1958 and was still influential in high political circles, that they had come to serve as bodyguards, they kidnapped him. The abduction and, on June 1, execution of so prominent a leader introduced to Argentina a group—at the time numbering only twelve members—known as the Montoneros. Taking their name from the bands of *gauchos* (cowboys) who had fought for rural *caudillos* (chieftains) during the 1800s, the Montoneros were, as their first communiqué declared, a particularly Argentine and Peronist movement. Originally an offshoot of Falangist youth groups, the Montoneros' founders moved to the Left as they came under the influence of radical Catholic priests who propagated the newly ascendant theology of liberation and the ideas of the Colombian guerrilla-priest Camilo Torres. They tended to see revolution in terms of national liberation rather than class struggle, and their ideology was informed by radical Catholic notions of social justice rather than pure or orthodox political doctrines such as Marxism-Leninism or Guevarism.

As evidenced in the name of their movement, the Montoneros drew on historic imagery and myth from the metaphors and symbols of the Argentine past. They acted out, in their Robin Hood–type field operations—strikes against banks, military outposts, and the like—fulfilling the most romantic and psychologically evocative of national stereotypes. Their very motto encapsulated their fierce intransigence: *Todo o Nada* (All or Nothing). Such a volatile and contradictory admixture of nationalism, Catholic populism, and commitment to direct action gravitated to revolutionary Peronism—with Perón himself as the focal point.

Perón, at the time of the emergence of the Montoneros, was in the closing years of his Spanish exile, maneuvering to return to Argentina. In their communiqué following the kidnapping and assassination of Aramburu, the Montoneros called on the people to resist the government of General Juan Carlos Onganía and to support the return of Perón.

The Montoneros saw Perón as a socialist leader in their own mold and justified their use of violence in large part using Perón's own statements on resistance and revolutionary war. Perón, still in Spain, accepted their support. He endorsed the movement's actions and in effect gave them carte blanche support for further violent measures. Though he did not endorse their assertion that revolutionary war was "the fundamental axis and motor of Peronism," he unabashedly praised urban guerrillas by calling them a "marvellous youth which every day unequivocally demonstrates its capacity and greatness. ... I have absolute faith in our lads who have learnt how to die for their ideals" (Gillespie 1982: 40). Correspondence with the leader, as well as Perón's public statements, convinced the Montoneros, as well as the Juventud Peronista movement, that Perón was committed to the goal of a socialist homeland. It was a naive belief that was to die hard, despite Perón's later denunciations. Although Perón had been willing to use the Montoneros as leverage for his return and as a mechanism for keeping Peronism's other factions in line during his absence, once back in Argentina he began to denounce revolutionary violence and to call for a return to orthodox Peronism within the now polarized Justicialista (Peronist) movement.

Still, in the short term Aramburu's assassination garnered the Montoneros popular support among the Peronist rank and file, and Perón's subsequent endorsement of that action contributed greatly to a precipitous leap in numbers. Thus, in 1971, when Mario Firmenich assumed leadership after the violent deaths of founders Fernando Abal Medina and Carlos Gustavo Ramus, along with their successor Sabino Navarro, the Montoneros counted only a few dozen members. Soon, Peronist factions that had snubbed the Montoneros in the past sought to merge with them. By far the largest addition to their ranks came from the support of the Juventud Peronista-Regional organizations, which became the Montoneros' legal front.

The Montoneros' continued raids and actions, as well as their growing popular support, eventually brought down the Onganía government. On June 8, 1972, the military replaced Onganía with an interim president and agreed to new elections. The increasing polarization of the country made it clear to the military that it would have to allow the return of Perón as a possible unifying figure. In March 1973, Héctor Cámpora, a virtual stand-in for Perón—who was not allowed to run—was elected by an overwhelming margin.

The Juventud Peronista, exalted by the turn of events, was sure its moment had arrived. The group pressured Cámpora to sign an amnesty for political prisoners and organized armed takeovers of government offices, factories, schools, universities, and radio and TV stations. Juventud Peronista leader Rodolfo Galimberti announced plans to form "popular militias" and to crush the union bureaucracy.

Perón was infuriated by these developments and snubbed Cámpora when he came to Spain to escort him home. He had been negotiating with many of his former enemies since 1970, and the 1973 winning ticket was actually a coalition of splinters of many political groups, in addition to the fractious Peronists themselves. As the more-or-less openly acknowledged power behind the throne, Perón returned to Argentina with an essentially caudillist outlook, despite his willingness to wheel and deal politically. But the Peronism he returned to was different from the one he had left—as was the nation itself. Polarization that had before been played out between Peronists and anti-Peronists had now become a menacing presence within the seething Peronist movement itself. The conflict manifested itself immediately upon Perón's return from exile on June 21, 1973, when a pitched battle broke out between left-wing Montoneros and their allies and right-wing Peronist factions, who had all gone to Ezeiza International Airport to greet the leader. Although the exact casualty figures will likely never be known, perhaps as many as 200, mainly leftists, were killed.

Perón quickly asserted that his sympathies in this power struggle did not lie with the Left. He commanded that revolutionary violence must now stop as Peronism regained power.

With Perón back, the Peronist unions threatened a general strike unless Perón himself ascended to power. On July 12, Cámpora resigned and new elections were called with Perón and his third wife, Isabel, composing the ticket. On September 23, Perón was elected president for the third time in his life.

Amazingly, the youthful Left continued to be naive about Perón's support and its position once he regained power. The leftists insisted that Perón was a socialist in their own image and maintained that anything he did to the contrary was merely a tactic. An oft-repeated joke of the period has Firmenich and a number of his comrades of the Peronist Left lined up about to be executed on Perón's orders by a firing squad of the Peronist Right. As the guns are leveled, Firmenich turns to the others and says, "So tell me—what do you think of this neat new tactic the Old Man has come up with?"

Thus, the Left ignored Perón's record of electoral solution, class conciliation and compromise, and firm opposition to Marxism-Leninism. To Perón, the Left was but a useful means of leverage and a check on the powerful unions.

Following the Ezeiza massacre, the Montoneros agreed to put down their arms and participate in the political process. The period of coexistence was short-lived, however. The assassination of labor leader and Perón ally José Rucci, generally attributed to the Montoneros, occurred just two days after Perón's election. In response to this event, Peronist leaders issued a document—signed by Perón—essentially declaring war on terrorist and Marxist groups that had infiltrated Peronism. Leftist violence, as well as right-wing paramilitary violence, increased.

With the economy in perpetual trouble and unrest boiling, the honeymoon was over practically before it began. Perón's health began to fail. The breaking point came on May Day at a traditional labor rally in the

Plaza de Mayo in front of the government palace. Members of the Montonero Left, still believing in their revolutionary camaraderie with Perón, mobilized perhaps 60,000 of the 100,000 in attendance, hoping to address the president directly and reestablish solidarity with him.

By the time Perón came to address the rally, the Montoneros had worked themselves into a fever pitch. They greeted him with chants of "What's going on general? Why is the people's government full of gorillas (right-wing elements)?" Perón cast aside his prepared speech about unity and berated the Left, calling them "stupid idiots" and "beardless wonders" (Gillespie 1982: 149, 150). In response, more than half the throng marched out as he spoke.

On September 6, the Montoneros returned underground to fight a popular war against the government of Isabel Perón, who had succeeded her husband upon his death on July 30. Their first major action after resuming warfare was the kidnapping of the Born brothers, Juan and Jorge, of the Bunge and Born multinational grain company, on September 19, 1974. They were released on June 20, 1975, after the grain company paid $60 million in ransom and distributed $1 million in clothing and food to the poor.

In 1975–1976 the Montoneros launched some of the largest guerrilla operations ever undertaken in Argentina, blowing up an Argentine Navy frigate missile launcher and a troop transport plane, taking over an airstrip, and attacking various military installations. They also continued their campaign of kidnapping and assassinating foreign business executives. The climate of violence, in which they were joined by the Ejército Revolucionario del Pueblo, destabilized the already inept government of Isabel Perón and was a factor in prompting the military coup of March 1976.

Following the coup, the military goal of eliminating subversion and the doctrine of messianic anti-Communism that surrounded it unleashed a period of repression between 1976 and 1983 that came to be known as *La Guerra Sucia* (The Dirty War), in which an estimated 30,000 people disappeared. The strategy of the military went far beyond any immediate security threat, encompassing practically the whole of Argentine society. Some observers estimate that for every one person who disappeared, another four were tortured.

In the face of this ferocity, the Montoneros were virtually decimated as a fighting force by 1977. By 1979, armed resistance came to a complete halt when a counteroffensive by guerrillas who had secretly returned from exile resulted in the almost total annihilation of these forces. It was estimated that by 1980, no more than 350 active Montoneros remained.

Beginning in 1980, nonviolent methods became the rule. "To resist is to win" became the watchword. The Montoneros never acknowledged defeat, though they were almost completely routed. In 1979, a political rupture among the Montoneros in exile further disintegrated the group.

After the 1983 return to democracy, several Montoneros were put on trial in 1985 by the Raúl Alfonsín government for "crimes" dating back to 1973. Firmenich, in exile in Brazil, was captured and eventually extradited during this period. Although he stood trial and was sentenced to life imprisonment, he was released in 1991 as a result of the late 1990 pardon issued by President Carlos Saúl Menem.

UTURUNCOS
Tiger-Men

First guerrilla group active in Argentina; operated briefly from 1959 to 1960 in the northwestern province of Tucumán; Peronist, Castrist; led by Enrique Mena.

The Uturuncos were the first guerrilla group active in Argentina. They were directly inspired by the triumph of the Cuban revolution and engaged in rural guerrilla warfare between 1959 and 1960 in the province of Tucumán in northwestern Argentina. Uturunco means "tiger-man" in the Quechua language. The members of this group were mostly former militants of the Alianza Libertadora Revolucionaria (Revolutionary Liberating Alliance) and the Partido Socialista de la Revolución Nacional (Socialist Party of the National Revolution).

In 1959, the Peronist movement was reorganizing under the leadership of John William Cooke, personal envoy of the exiled Juan Domingo Perón. At the same time, a group of young men set up the Uturunco movement near the Cerro Cochuna in the province of Tucumán. They were directed by Enrique Mena, who came to be known as their commander.

The movement demanded the resignation of President Arturo Frondizi of the Radical Party, even though Frondizi advocated agreement with Peronism, the annulment of the oil contracts the government had signed with foreign companies, and the return of Perón. The group sought to match up a general offensive with workers' militancy, military uprising, and the multiplication of rural Peronist guerrilla units.

Bibliographical Commentary

As one of the two best-organized and -financed guerrilla groups in the hemisphere, the Montoneros and the Ejército Revolucionario del Pueblo have been the focus of considerable analysis. Richard Gillespie's *Soldiers of Peron: Argentina's Montoneros* provides an excellent comprehensive critical history of the movement from a sympathetic but nonpartisan tone, with abundant information culled from interviews and guerrilla documents. A more emotional account is offered in *Montoneros: La soberbia armada*, by Pablo Giussani. *Todo o nada*, by Maria Seoane, provides a lucid treatment of the ERP experience. Although the main theme of Donald Hodges's erudite *Argentina's 'Dirty War': An Intellectual Biography* is not the guerrilla groups per se, his detailed study of the sociopolitical context of Argentina includes substantial information about the Montoneros and the ERP as well as data about the smaller groups. James Kohl's *Urban Guerrilla Warfare in Latin America* also contains information about lesser organizations and reproduces several guerrilla documents. Kohl includes extremely useful chronologies for quick reference. João Batista Berardo's *Guerrilhas e guerrilheiros no drama da América Latina* serves to fill in gaps about smaller groups, but its intense ideological bias and disorganized presentation detract from the work's usefulness.

2

BOLIVIA

EJERCITO DE LIBERACION NACIONAL (ELN)
Army of National Liberation

Led by Ernesto "Che" Guevara, Roberto "Coco" Peredo, and Guido "Inti" Peredo; operated from July/August 1966 to October/November 1967 in southwest Santa Cruz, a southeastern province of Bolivia, and until 1970 near La Paz and in Alto Beni; Marxist and *foquista* (using foco theory as a revolutionary tactic, whereby a small nucleus, or "foco," in the countryside sets off other hot spots of rebellion); supported by the Cuban government.

Ernesto "Che" Guevara's aspirations to export the Cuban experience and spark revolution throughout Latin America began in 1963–1964 near Salta in northwestern Argentina. By 1965, he had begun traveling to various parts of the Communist world to study guerrilla strategy. The Ejército de Liberación Nacional was the instrument to promote revolutionary struggle in the hemisphere, with Bolivia as the first stage of the insurrection.

The landlocked South American nation was chosen for this type of activity, among other reasons, because of the success of its revolution of 1952, led by the Movimiento Nacionalista Revolucionario (Nationalist Revolutionary Movement), and because of the overall poverty of the population, approximately 60 percent of which was illiterate. In addition, 70 percent of the population was indigenous and rural. The economy was heavily dependent on tin mining. Since their nationalization in 1952 the tin mines were working profitably, although labor conflict was persistent and profound. Still, the government of General René Barrientos, which took power in 1964, had declared "austerity" in everything except economic development.

Guevara arrived in Bolivia in November 1966 and spent his first two months establishing contacts in Argentina and Peru and strengthening

23

urban Bolivian networks. He attempted to build his Bolivian network through Mario Monje, secretary general of the pro-Soviet Partido Comunista Boliviano (PCB, Bolivian Communist Party), but the two were unable to reach an agreement. Among their numerous differences were their attitudes toward the Soviet-Chinese Communist Party split—while Monje supported the USSR, Guevara's preference for neutrality was in line with Castro's. Also, the PCB did not subscribe to Guevara's foco theory of guerrilla warfare. The PCB's refusal to cooperate remained consistent until the ELN's catastrophic defeat, even though "Coco" Peredo had been a member of the PCB's Central Committee.

The only organizational support the guerrillas were able to obtain was from Moisés Guevara, a pro-Chinese tin miners' leader in Oruro. By the end of January 1967 they had decided that Moisés Guevara's group should be absorbed into the ELN that February.

In the meantime, the group of Cubans and Bolivians who formed the ELN were being trained as soldiers at the base in Camiri, a rugged jungle area about 400 miles southeast of La Paz. After constructing the camp and digging supply caves, Guevara led twenty-seven men on a six-week training march beginning on February 1. During the course of the month they went north, talking to peasants and charting territory.

At around that time, the Bolivian military became aware of the ELN's existence. Two miners who had been recruited by the guerrillas fled with a .22 caliber rifle that they tried to sell in a town. Police and army security forces questioned them about the weapon, and the miners eventually revealed that they had come from a guerrilla training camp. A patrol spotted the camp from a distance a few days later.

ELN military action began on the morning of March 23, 1967, with an ambush of a Bolivian patrol along the Ñancahuazú river gorge. At that time the forces were made up of forty-one fighters—seventeen Cubans, twenty Bolivians, three Peruvians, plus Che Guevara. The operation was deemed a success, as the guerrillas killed eleven soldiers and took seven prisoners, but the group was not prepared to wage war. They were too few, too isolated, and too exhausted. Furthermore, they failed to gain the support of the local population. Peasants considered the ELN foreigners and intruders.

In April, following another guerrilla victory, Washington became involved in the conflict, sending aid, weapons, and military experts. Colonel Joseph P. Rile and Major Robert "Peppy" Sheldon headed a six-month-long antiguerrilla school to train a 600-member Bolivian special forces unit that would later play a part in defeating the ELN.

On April 15 and 16, as the ELN was traveling south to Muyupampa, Guevara made a crucial decision to split the group. He would continue ahead with twenty-seven able-bodied men, and a fourteen-member rear guard, consisting of ill fighters, would be led by a Cuban with the nom de guerre Joaquín (real name: Juan Nuñez, a member of the Cuban Communist Party and one of the first to join Castro's guerrillas in Sierra Maestra). The two groups never reunited and spent the remainder of the year in search of each other.

By the end of May the guerrillas had become a media sensation, particularly because of the episode involving French philosopher and journalist Régis Debray. Debray arrived at the guerrilla camp in March in order to interview Guevara, only to be forced to leave the site along with two other journalists when the military action began. Nevertheless, the three were imprisoned as guerrillas. Debray's imprisonment generated impressive international publicity, as did his book *Defensa en Camiri* (Defense at Camiri).

Both guerrilla groups continued to move in June and July, occasionally clashing with the military. Their greatest setback occurred in August, when two young guerrillas deserted and led Bolivian army units to the ELN supply caves on the Ñancahuazú. The guerrillas were thus isolated and without arms, food, and medicine. Joaquín lost one man on July 1 in a clash with the army and another in a clash on August 10, during which two men were captured, leaving eleven members in the group.

In mid-August Joaquín's and Guevara's forces both coincidentally approached the house of a peasant they had encountered earlier in the year. Soldiers disguised as peasants alerted the army, and on August 31 the eleven members of Joaquín's band were killed while crossing a river. Guevara's group, which arrived shortly after, took over Alto Seco, a small village to the west, on September 24. By then, having lost men in successive clashes with the army, they numbered twenty-one. Two days later, three of the guerrillas died in a clash with the army and one was captured. This was the beginning of the end, as the 600 "Ranger" troops trained by the U.S. officers saturated the area.

The remaining seventeen guerrillas, including Guevara, were surrounded in Higueras, and on October 8, they again prepared to attack. They divided in an attempt to break through the encircling army, but four were killed in the Quebrada del Yuro and two were captured along with Guevara, only to be later executed. Four held out until October 14, when they were captured and killed. Five of the six members of the group led by "Inti" Peredo managed to make it to Cochabamba—three Cubans who returned to Cuba via Chile and two Bolivians (including "Inti" Peredo) who returned to their homes.

Because he was a survivor of Guevara's group, Peredo acquired influence throughout Latin America as an ideological theorist. He became Guevara's successor as head of the movement and planned to launch a new foco in Alto Beni in 1970, but he was murdered at the home of a Communist militant on September 8, 1969. However, the plan was carried out by his brother "Chato" in July 1970 with funds provided by the Uruguayan Tupamaros.

The group, made up of some fifty fighters (Peruvians, Chileans, and Brazilians in addition to Bolivians), attacked a mining community seventy-five miles northeast of La Paz and kidnapped two engineers. The captives were exchanged for ten political prisoners, who were flown to Cuba. But the guerrillas were decimated in the subsequent clashes with the armed forces, and Chato was captured in October. Under an amnesty declared by the regime of General Juan José Torres, the ELN survivors were offered safe conduct out of the country if they surrendered and went into exile. A group of eight men left for Chile, invited by that country's newly elected president, Salvador Allende.

The ELN became active again in the early 1970s, during the military government headed by Hugo Banzer. However, with significant financial assistance provided by the Brazilian government, the Bolivian military was successful in repressing ELN activities.

A cell of the ELN resurfaced yet one more time toward the end of the 1980s. It called itself the ELN/Comando Néstor Paz Zamora (ELN/Néstor Paz Zamora Commando), in honor of a dead guerrilla who also happened to be the brother of then President Jaime Paz Zamora, who had come to power in 1989. The group was responsible for the death of two U.S. Mormon missionaries in May 1989 and the kidnapping of Jorge Lonsdale, the president of the Bolivian subsidiary of Coca-Cola, in December 1990. Lonsdale was killed when security forces clashed with guerrillas after surrounding the house where Lonsdale was being held. After this bloody episode, Bolivian security forces managed to crush all guerrilla activity.

Bibliographical Commentary

In his comprehensive *Guerrilla Movements in Latin America*, Richard Gott devotes substantial attention to Che Guevara's Ejército de Liberación Nacional, tracing developments from the Sino-Soviet split and its effect on the revolutionary Left in Bolivia. Gott combines an eminently readable storytelling style with abundant references to primary documents and sources. Luis Mercier Vega concentrates more on the Bolivian campaign in *Guerrillas in Latin America: The Technique of Counter-State*. *Guerrilhas e guerrilheiros no drama da América Latina*, by João Batista Berardo, and *Diez años de insurrección en América Latina*, by Vania Bambirra, Alvaro Lopez, Moisés Moleiro, Silvestre Condoruma, Carlos Nuñez, Ruy Mauro Marini, and Antonio Zapata, both highly biased treatments of the guerrilla phenomenon with excessive use of leftist rhetoric, can nevertheless be used for corroborating names, dates, and other facts. *Latin American Revolutionaries: Groups, Goals, Methods*, by Michael Radu and Vladimir Tismaneanu, which suffers from extreme right-wing ideological distortion, can be consulted for the same purpose. In his *The Latin American Revolution: Politics and Strategy from Apro-Marxism to Guevarism*, Donald C. Hodges fills in with seldom-looked-at information about the ELN after Guevara's death and the subsequent activities of the Peredo brothers. Finally, Gary Prado Salmón, in his *The Defeat of Che Guevara: Military Response to Guerrilla Challenge in Bolivia* and Richard Harris, in *Death of a Revolutionary: Che Guevara's Last Mission* offer two riveting accounts of the last days of Che Guevara and his followers.

3

BRAZIL

ACAO LIBERTADORA NACIONAL (ALN)
National Liberating Action

Initiated activities in 1968; operated mainly in Rio de Janeiro, São Paulo, and Belo Horizonte; Marxist; led by Carlos Marighella, who was killed in 1969, and Joaquim Câmara Ferreira; supported itself through bank robberies and kidnappings; most daring coup was the kidnapping of U.S. ambassador Charles Burke Elbrik in 1969; active until around 1971.

João Goulart was elected vice president of Brazil in 1954 and ascended to the presidency in 1960 after the resignation of the incumbent, Janio Quadros. Even as Brazil was drifting toward economic collapse, Goulart, a populist leader, continued to promise unrealistic reforms, such as controlling the country's runaway 8 percent monthly inflation rate. Faced with an increasingly skeptical Congress, in 1964 Goulart attempted to force his policies through by presidential decree. The resulting outrage of the armed forces culminated in a coup d'état that replaced Goulart with a military regime under the command of General Humberto Castelo Branco.

The 1964 coup began a trend toward an increasing concentration of military power. Congress was systematically weakened and repressive measures, including arbitrary arrests, were widely used by police and paramilitary forces. On December 13, 1968, Castelo Branco's successor, Marshal Arturo da Costa e Silva, declared institutional Act No. 5, which effectively concentrated all executive power in the president. The new leader justified this measure as a means of suppressing activities that could destabilize domestic order. A virtual terrorist state followed in which torture and abuse of power became common.

The year 1968 also marked the beginning of at least ten organized urban guerrilla groups and a handful of splinter factions. The Açao Libertadora Nacional, however, was one of only a few that had even a marginal influence on Brazilian politics at the time. The founder of the group, Carlos Marighella, joined the Partido Comunista Brasileiro (PCB, Brazilian Communist Party) at the age of sixteen in 1928 and left school to devote more time to political agitation. The son of a black Brazilian woman and an Italian immigrant, he was arrested several times and even briefly held a seat in the Federal Chamber of Deputies until the PCB was again outlawed in 1947. Marighella then returned to clandestinity, this time for good.

After the coup, he became devoted to the idea of a violent revolution to overthrow the current regime and criticized the PCB for supporting the concept of peaceful resistance. Marighella resigned from the party's executive committee and, after traveling to Cuba to attend the Organization of Latin American Solidarity Conference in 1967—in violation of a party ban—he finally abandoned the PCB altogether. It was in February 1968 that Marighella founded the ALN, which never reached a maximum estimated strength of more than 200 members.

Upon his return to Brazil, Marighella began to form small action groups and outline his revolutionary program. He subscribed to the principle that the political and military branches of the movement should be one and the same, and he rejected the foco theory because it gave priority to the rural over the urban guerrilla.

The majority of Marighella's recruits were university students or intellectuals in their late teens and twenties. The remainder were military deserters or other Communist dissidents such as Joaquim Câmara Ferreira, who would later lead the movement. The movement also received support and asylum from radical members of the clergy.

For most of the first year of the ALN's existence, its activities were limited to bank robberies and raids on military barracks to acquire resources. Occasionally these crimes had a political motive, as in the theft of $2.4 million in funds earmarked for corrupt activity, but Marighella originally intended them to be only an initial phase in order to finance subsequent rural operations. More than 100 banks were robbed by the ALN and the other groups that formed in its wake. Marighella's followers also dynamited army barracks and warehouses owned by U.S. companies, occupied radio stations to broadcast revolutionary proclamations, and freed a group of jailed comrades from a prison in Rio. However, the ALN soon found itself limited to the urban centers of Rio and São Paulo.

In June 1969, Marighella wrote the *Minimanual of the Urban Guerrilla,* which has been highly influential as a handbook for terrorist groups owing to its precise information concerning such modern techniques as plane hijacking and bomb threats. In it the tactics of the ALN and many of its goals are described. The movement was to have had several stages, beginning with urban terrorism and progressing into the rural areas in order to gather the peasants into a unified front that would then topple the ruling regime. The urban groups would be completely autonomous, compartmentalized, and fueled by individual motivation. This plan resulted, however, in sporadic and isolated crimes, and as a result the ALN was frequently confused with common bandits.

Marighella was often criticized for his fervent endorsement of violence. In the *Minimanual,* he outlines the use of firearms, explosives, and assassinations, stating, "The urban guerrilla's reason for existence, the basic condition in which he acts and survives, is to shoot" (Kohl 1974: 97). He aimed, however, to maintain the favor of the people. He restricted the methods to ones that would incite public sympathy and deflect government retaliation. Marighella avoided associating the movement with a political credo and concerned his manifestos with the eventual overthrow of the government.

Owing to a variety of causes, not the least of them being the titanic task of organizing the country's remote peasants, the ALN was unable to exert more than a minor influence on national politics during its life span. Soon, the ALN's tactics progressed to selective assassinations and culminated in the kidnapping of several foreign ambassadors who were held until fellow revolutionaries were released from prison and flown to asylum. The first victim of this strategy was U.S. ambassador Charles Burke Elbrik, who was abducted on September 4, 1969, through a joint action by the ALN and another guerrilla group, the Movimento Revolucionario de Outubre 8 (MR-8, October 8th Revolutionary Movement), and released three days later after a manifesto was published and fifteen political prisoners were freed.

After this unexpected act of subversion, the government reinstated the death penalty, which had been abolished since 1891, and embarked on a wave of counterinsurgency measures that seriously affected the ALN. With the arrest of two Dominican friars, the police were able to dismantle the guerrilla network. On November 4, 1969, Marighella was trapped and killed in a police ambush on a street in São Paulo.

Marighella's successor, Câmara Ferreira, was partially responsible for the subsequent kidnappings of the West German ambassador Ehrenfried von Holleben and the Swiss ambassador Giovanni Bucher in 1970. The price for the release of these diplomats was forty and seventy prisoners, respectively.

The ALN, like other leftist Brazilian movements, drastically weakened and dissolved after 1970. It was only through combined efforts and attempted mergers that urban guerrillas were able to maintain their terrorist activities and function with a decreasing amount of recruits. The disparate factions were never able to agree on a unifying strategy, and their public profile dwindled in the face of an increasingly repressive and brutal regime.

On October 23, 1970, Câmara Ferreira was arrested, tortured, and killed. The ALN, now virtually leaderless and splintered into numerous other factions, suffered a final series of arrests and murders. Although guerrilla activity continued sporadically in Brazil into the early 1970s under the banner of the ALN, the movement was essentially finished.

MOVIMIENTO REVOLUCIONARIO DE OUTUBRE 8 (MR-8)
October 8th Revolutionary Movement

Active in the late 1960s; operated mainly in the state of Rio Grande do Sul; Guevarist; cooperated with the ALN to kidnap U.S. ambassador Charles Burke Elbrik in 1969; led by Jorge Medeiros do Vale.

The Movimiento Revolucionario de Outubre 8 was founded in the late 1960s by dissident members of the pro-Soviet Partido Comunista Brasileiro. It took its name from the date revolutionary Ernesto "Che" Guevara was captured in Bolivia, October 8, 1967.

The main reason for the split was the dissidents' conviction that armed struggle was the only viable revolutionary method. They criticized the passive resistance politics of the PCB leadership vis-à-vis the repressive military regimes that took over the country after the overthrow of President João Goulart in 1964, advocated urban guerrilla theory, and cooperated with other terrorist groups in organizing kidnappings. The organization's strength never exceeded 100 cadres.

Its most spectacular operation, carried out in cooperation with the ALN, was the kidnapping of U.S. ambassador Charles Burke Elbrik in downtown Rio de Janeiro. The diplomat was exchanged for fifteen political prisoners.

Like the other, more powerful Brazilian guerrilla groups, the ALN and the Vanguardia Popular Revolucionaria (VPR, Popular Revolutionary Vanguard), the MR-8 weakened and dissolved in the early 1970s.

VANGUARDIA POPULAR REVOLUCIONARIA (VPR)
Popular Revolutionary Vanguard

Initiated activities in 1968 in the state of Guanabara and a few large surrounding cities; originally left-wing nationalist, Castrist later; led by Onofre Pinto, Carlos Lamarca, and Ladislas Dowbor (aka "Nelson" or "Jamil"); supported itself by robberies and Cuban funds; crumbled in the late 1970s.

Most active in the 1960s, the Vanguardia Popular Revolucionaria was one of the groups that argued that Brazil's military regime would not tolerate conventional methods of protest and that armed action was therefore the only viable option. After the overthrow of populist president João Goulart in 1964, constitutional rights had been suspended and Brazil was ruled by a succession of three generals: Humberto Castelo Branco, Arturo da Costa e Silva, and Emilio Garrastazu Medici.

The VPR's economic program was inspired by the Cuban revolution and consisted of the basic Marxist-Leninist economic objectives: agrarian reform, expropriation of big companies, and nationalization of foreign companies. The group, which at one point numbered several hundred fighters, attempted to create in Brazil the basis for a further continental fulfillment of socialist revolution. By its own admission, it oriented its armed actions in such a way as to make them politically profitable and believed that by spreading armed action it was deepening the understanding of the struggle among the masses. It was more successful in urban than in rural warfare.

The founders were members of a small left-wing organization of former army officers. In the late 1960s, its leader was a black ex-army sergeant, Onofre Pinto. In 1969, a respected army captain, Carlos Lamarca, deserted the Fourth Infantry Regiment with seventy light machine guns and joined the VPR. Ironically, Lamarca, an excellent shot, had been picked by the government to teach bank tellers how to shoot holdup terrorists. Lamarca also was a U.S.-trained expert in counterinsurgency techniques.

The VPR guerrillas were convinced that the struggle to topple the established order would take a long time. To secure funds, they participated in kidnappings and bank robberies and stole small arms, dynamite, and machine guns from garrisons. In addition, they were supplied with some arms from Cuba. The group also stole cars for revolutionary purposes (according to VPR ideologue Ladislas Dowbor, these vehicles were always returned to their owners with a tank full of gas).

Then came the police crackdown. At the end of March 1969, Pinto was caught and Lamarca became the leader of the movement. One month later, Lamarca, Dowbor, and ten others attacked a military police barracks in the factory district of São Caetano do Sul. In April, Dowbor was arrested by police and tortured. His lawyer managed to obtain his release because Dowbor had never been formally charged.

In March 1970, the VPR kidnapped a Japanese consul, Nobuo Okuchi, on the streets of São Paulo. Three days later, he was released in exchange for five political prisoners, who were sent to Mexico. After this kidnapping, the movement faced serious setbacks. It suffered defections and betrayals because of differences of opinion on tactical issues concerning rural versus urban guerrilla warfare. It also took significant losses. Juarez Guimarães de Brito, considered a top VPR ideologist, was killed in May 1970, and Lamarca died in a shootout in 1971. The rural guerrilla base that Lamarca had attempted to set up earlier in the year in Ribeira crumbled as well. Dowbor, who had been arrested again, was among those VPR militants who had been granted asylum in Algeria in a prisoner exchange for the kidnapped German ambassador, Ehrenfried von Holleben, in 1970.

As a result, both the VPR and its splinter group, the Vanguardia Armada Revolucionaria—Palmares (VAR, Armed Revolutionary Vanguard), were considerably reduced in size and importance and unable to recover from Lamarca's demise. Former VPR militants who were active within the VAR-Palmares were arrested by the authorities in 1978.

Bibliographical Commentary

While clearly sympathetic to the guerrilla cause, James Kohl lucidly analyzes the theoretical positions and activities of Brazilian guerrilla groups in *Urban Guerrilla Warfare in Latin America*. A detailed sociopolitical backdrop is provided, as well as a chronology covering events from 1964 to 1973. In *Urban Guerrillas*, Robert Moss uses a balanced, factual approach framed in historical background to discuss the Brazilian guerrilla experience, devoting the bulk of one chapter to the ALN and considering the lesser groups only in relationship to Marighella's outfit. The account contains no references to documents or primary sources. For a succinct but well-presented general overview, consult Raymond Estep's

Guerrilla Warfare in Latin America, 1963–1975. Most of the material available is devoted to the ALN, and information about the lesser groups is scarcer. Because of its influence and the militant tone of its rhetoric, which constitutes a typical example of the "voice" of hemispheric guerrillas, Marighella's *Minimanual of the Urban Guerrilla* makes for particularly insightful reading. Contemporary popular press accounts from prestigious publications like the *New York Times* and *The Economist* are useful in cross-referencing data.

4

CHILE

FRENTE PATRIOTICO MANUEL RODRIGUEZ/
PARTIDO COMUNISTA DE CHILE (FPMR/PCC)
Manuel Rodríguez Patriotic Front/
Communist Party of Chile

Active from the early 1980s to the present but gave up armed struggle at the end of the military regime of General Augusto Pinochet; armed branch of the Marxist Partido Comunista de Chile; led by Manuel Huerta; numbered 1,000 at its maximum strength; supported by the Soviet bloc, Cuba, Nicaragua; attempted to assassinate President Pinochet in 1986.

The founding father of the Partido Comunista de Chile (Communist Party of Chile), Luis Emilio Recabarren, believed in a government controlled by workers' unions rather than political parties. In 1912, Recabarren founded the Partido Socialista de los Trabajadores (PST, Socialist Workers' Party) in Iquique. By 1919 it had evolved from a simple labor union to an organized revolutionary force, breaking relations with the U.S.-based Industrial Workers of the World and associating itself with the Moscow-based Red International of Unions.

Recabarren had been elected to parliament in 1916 but was not allowed to take his seat because of his political ideas. He was elected again in 1921 on the platform of educating the working class and the poor. Although not immediately successful, Recabarren introduced the labor movement as a political topic in Chile and traveled around the nation forming newspapers to get his message to the people.

In the PST's Fourth Congress in January 1922 in Rancagua, it decided to officially affiliate itself with the Third International and change its name to Partido Comunista de Chile. It was several years until Moscow formally accepted the PCC into full membership in the Third International, although the PCC had already accepted Lenin's "21 points" necessary for membership. In 1922 Recabarren traveled to Russia and returned with new Leninist ideas—transition to a socialist state via a peaceful road, using parliamentary democracy rather than violence to achieve revolutionary goals.

Although the PCC had sympathizers throughout the nation, its main political support traditionally came from the northern working-class mining and industrial sectors in towns with populations of 30,000–60,000 people, and until the 1930s it was almost synonymous with the trade union movement.

Military dictator Carlos Ibañez del Campo was the first Chilean president to outlaw the PCC, which he did in 1927. He also attempted to crush the unions and repress the opposition. These efforts caused the PCC to become more radical, and on December 13, 1924, over the objections of Recabarren, six ultraleftists were elected to the PCC's Executive Committee. Six days later, realizing the party no longer supported his ideas, Recabarren committed suicide.

The ban on the PCC was lifted in 1931, but the 1930s became a time of infighting among PCC members. The Soviet Stalin-Trotsky fight in the USSR caused some members to leave the party and Trotskyist Manuel Hidalgo Plaza to form the Communist Left Party.

The PCC was once again outlawed in February 1937. It was legalized in 1938, but in 1948 it was outlawed yet a third time and PCC leader Luis Corvalán was imprisoned. Seven years later, he was jailed again after the party sponsored its first general strike. Because of this arrest, the PCC adopted a new strategy of pressuring the government by working within the system. In 1961, Corvalán was elected to the senate. The PCC's popularity continued to grow, and in 1969, it won 22 of the 150 seats in the National Chamber of Deputies, or 17.3 percent, up from 12.73 percent in 1965.

In 1970, the PCC joined the Unidad Popular coalition in support of Salvador Allende Gossens, who became the first democratically elected socialist president in the Western Hemisphere. But public support for Allende waned when his government failed to sustain the initial gains for Chile's poor, and eventually he was overthrown on September 11, 1973, by General Augusto Pinochet.

The failure of the Allende government was a crushing blow to the party, and in 1980 it revised its ideology of peaceful struggle. As a result of this restructuring, that same year the PCC formed the Frente Patriótico Manuel Rodríguez to serve as its armed militia. The FPMR, named after a guerrilla leader of the independence era, had two related objectives: to force the military dictatorship to relinquish power and to foster a workers' revolution.

PCC secretary Luis Corvalán stated in 1979 that terrorism would find a "wide open field" in Chile and proclaimed a new era of violence with the establishment of the FPMR (Whelan 1989: 665). The PCC broke relations with the terrorist FPMR in the early 1980s, however, to gain legitimacy and to build broad political support from other leftist and centrist parties.

The FPMR's first terrorist actions came in 1980. Its leaders believed that if they could not undermine the armed forces and Carabinero national police force, its struggle would never succeed. The FPMR sponsored violence in many forms, including sabotage, assassinations, strikes, mass demonstrations, and disruption of high school and university activities. The organization came into the public eye on March 7–8, 1984, when members forcibly occupied a radio station and read a statement denouncing President Augusto Pinochet, who had come to power through a military coup on September 11, 1973, ousting socialist president Salvador Allende Gossens.

During the first three months of 1984, the FPMR sponsored more than 130 bombings, which at times cut off electricity to up to two-thirds of the country. On March 23 the government fought back and declared a ninety-day state of emergency, the first in seven years, during which 600 leftists were arrested. These bombings spurred Congress to strengthen Chile's antiterrorist laws. A new measure, passed on May 15, reinstated the death penalty for those found guilty of terrorist assassinations.

The terrorist activities, however, continued. In 1984 alone, the FPMR sponsored more than 1,100 bombings and 350 other attacks. From 1984 to 1986 more than 600 Chileans died or were wounded in 3,326 bombings, 1,889 acts of sabotage, 649 armed assaults, and 162 kidnappings and assassination attempts by the FPMR and other terrorist organizations.

Throughout 1985 the FPMR sponsored numerous bombings of railway lines of U.S.-based multinational corporations and of power stations, knocking out electricity all over the nation. Government security forces discovered an FPMR arsenal in the northern city of Vallenar in 1985. It consisted of 3,000 automatic rifles, 275 rocket launchers, 2 million rounds of ammunition, and tons of explosives. This discovery fueled Pinochet's fear of terrorism in Chile and led to a severe government backlash against the Left.

The FPMR continued its actions throughout 1986, which it called the "decisive" year, carrying out holdups and assassinations of government forces and the national police (Whelan 1989: 834). In August 1986 the Chilean security forces uncovered the FPMR's Carrizal arsenal, the largest ever found in Latin America. The arsenal consisted of seventy tons of munitions valued at $30 million from the Soviet Union, Nicaragua, and Cuba. Discovered in the seizure were 3,400 M-16 rifles, 117 Soviet rocket launchers, 179 antitank rockets, 3.5 million rounds for automatic rifles, machine guns, FN-FL assault rifles, submachine guns, and vehicles. Government forces also discovered several safe houses and arrested thirty-six key FPMR personnel. Secret operations plans discovered during the raid had been worked on for more than a year. The discovery seriously curtailed the FPMR's clandestine activities.

On September 7, 1986, the FPMR carried out "Operation Twentieth Century" to assassinate Pinochet, its boldest attack ever, in the belief that the only way to overthrow the regime was to kill Pinochet himself. The attack involved seventy militants who monitored the president's armed motorcade traveling from his presidential mansion in Melocotón to Santiago. The rebels ambushed the motorcade with machine gun fire and antitank rockets. Although one rocket hit the Mercedes in which the president and his grandson were traveling, it failed to explode and the president escaped with only minor injuries to his left hand. In all, a total of five members of the motorcade were killed and another eleven wounded in the attack.

Following the assassination attempt, government forces cracked down on the FPMR and around 40 percent of its members were captured. At least thirty rebels involved in the assassination attempt were arrested, nine of whom were sentenced to death. The crackdown was a near-fatal blow to the organization, which had to scale back its activities significantly. As the crackdown continued, on June 15, 1987, government forces discovered eight of the FPMR's safe houses. In this operation, eleven guerrillas were killed in one shootout. Documents found in the safe houses led to more FPMR arrests.

FPMR leaders were criticized for inadequate planning and training— one of the reasons that the attempt on Pinochet's life failed. To correct this problem, the FPMR sent a number of cadres to terrorism training camps in East Germany.

Although the PCC demanded that the FPMR cut back on its activities, the FPMR leadership refused and the organization continued to carry out bombings, kidnappings, and assassinations. These activities prompted additional counterattacks from government forces and increased the FPMR's pariah status with other leftists. The FPMR further alienated itself from public opinion—and caused the government to increase its retaliatory efforts—by disrupting the visit of Pope John Paul II in April 1987.

In 1988 the FPMR recruited members, stockpiled arms, and executed another series of subversive actions from its secret headquarters in Buenos Aires. To improve its image abroad, the organization opened information offices in Belgium, France, Italy, Spain, and Venezuela.

In January 1988, government forces came upon new FPMR arsenals in Temuco, Concepción, and Chillán. They also discovered that the FPMR had used a small plane to distribute arms to its members throughout the country. FPMR forces fought back by exploding four bombs in southern Concepción and bombing two banks in Santiago. One bomb detonated prematurely, killing three FPMR militants. Four bombs were also found in northern Coronel and Calama before they detonated. In addition, the FPMR tried to disrupt public transportation by burning minibuses in Santiago and Valparaíso.

The organization persisted in its campaign of mass violence until the end of the military regime and the democratic election of President Patricio Aylwin in 1990. It continues its activities to foster the workers' revolution, but now in a nonviolent manner.

MOVIMIENTO DE IZQUIERDA REVOLUCIONARIA (MIR)
Movement of the Revolutionary Left

Founded in 1965 and went underground in 1969; operated essentially in urban areas of Chile; strongly Castrist and Guevarist; led by Andrés Pascal Allende, Miguel Enríquez, Víctor Toro, Hernán Aquilo, and Arturo Villavella; its militants trained in Cuba and Hungary; supported itself through robberies and funds from its front organization, the Movimiento Democrático Popular; still seeks to establish socialist state.

The founders of the Movimiento de Izquierda Revolucionaria were firm believers in the Castrist and Guevarist brands of Marxism-Leninism.

After its foundation in 1965, the MIR embodied the radical Left in Chilean politics. It was an illegal, anti-imperialist, anticapitalist group committed to guerrilla warfare. It opposed all traditional leftist parties for not being truly revolutionary and considered political compromise a betrayal of its ideology. The MIR emphasized undermining the armed forces, destroying the "bourgeois legal superstructure," and installing a government of workers and peasants to lay the foundation for a socialist state (Whelan 1989: 254).

MIR guerrillas believed that these goals could only be accomplished through both armed and political class struggles of the masses throughout the nation. Obtaining funds through bank robberies, the organization assassinated political leaders, bombed public utilities, provoked armed confrontations with the military, attempted to gain control of territory, and organized a political structure to rule the nation.

In August 1965, the MIR held a constituent congress in which those in attendance—former members of the Partido Comunista de Chile (PCC, Communist Party of Chile), the Partido Socialista (Socialist Party), the Partido Revolucionario de los Trabajadores (Revolutionary Workers' Party), and the Vanguardia Marxista Revolucionaria (Revolutionary Marxist Vanguard)—elected their first general secretary, Enrique Sepúlveda.

Although in its first few years of existence it remained essentially a group of intellectuals, the MIR tried to generate revolutionary ideas among workers and peasants. It supported not only illegal land seizures without compensation but also propaganda campaigns and public manifestations, which it used for propaganda effect. The MIR received especially strong support from the impoverished Mapuche Indians, who carried out many of its land seizures in southern Temuco under its flag, and from students at the University of Concepción. In fact, the MIR operated in all eight autonomous universities of Chile.

In 1967, the MIR leadership gave priority to attracting peasants and the impoverished to its cause by placing propaganda in the publication *Punto Final*. It also increased the effectiveness of its cadres by training them in a camp outside Concepción. The government cracked down on the MIR that same year. The Carabinero national police force seized arms and explosives and arrested recruits in the MIR guerrilla training facility in Guayacán, near Santiago. By the end of the year, the MIR leadership had changed from intellectuals to combat trainers, including general secretary Miguel Enríquez, who emphasized grassroots terrorism and strategies to gain support from workers and peasants.

The MIR became a very strong organization, with some 2,000 militants and about 5,000 sympathizers. Between 1967 and 1970, it undertook at least fourteen armed actions, including robberies of supermarkets and banks to finance its operations, and a raid on a police post in the northern region of Copiapó. On June 6, 1969, MIR militants attacked Hernán Osses, publisher of the Talcahuano newspaper *Noticias de la Tarde*, after he announced that members of the group had kidnapped and beaten him. The government responded to Osses's allegations by swooping down on MIR supporters at the University of Concepción. This action constituted the first police raid on a Chilean university in fifty years.

The MIR went underground in 1969. Despite having its actions denounced by leftist parties, the organization became increasingly aggressive and influential. Also in the late 1960s, several small groups broke off from the MIR to form even more extremist organizations, including the Vanguardia Organizada del Pueblo (Organized Vanguard of the People).

The MIR supported the election of Socialist president Salvador Allende Gossens in 1970, suspending all armed actions three months before the election and allowing the Allende campaign to use its intelligence services to investigate the activities of the ultraright. The MIR had high hopes for the socialist government but soon became disenchanted because it wanted a more radical revolution than the one Allende was offering, including the abolition of parliament and its replacement with a People's Assembly and the takeover of all farms and industry without compensation. In fact, many MIR members saw the Allende election as a major defeat for the movement because it reduced the credibility of their contention that revolution could only be brought to Chile through violent means.

Under Allende, the MIR continued to carry out land seizures, bank robberies, arson attacks, kidnappings, hijackings, and infiltration of the military. It also advocated arming the people so they could defend the gains they had made under President Allende. The MIR's main targets were not so much the industrialists, who already were being attacked by Allende's government, but rather the small and medium-sized proprietors, whose farms were not included in the agrarian reform programs; houses built for workers' cooperatives, in their view the products of a bourgeois setup, not of the revolution and not truly revolutionary; and small and medium-sized factories, which had not been nationalized by Allende.

The MIR stated that it would give all the money gained from bank robberies to the peasants and workers by "investing it to arm and organize the cadres necessary to return to all the workers" what had been "stolen from them" by Chile's owner class (Whelan 1989: 253).

Initially, Allende looked favorably upon the MIR, believing that if he legalized subversive groups and ignored their illegal activities he could ensure that they would not rise up against the government. In line with this way of thinking, after taking office he ordered that charges filed during the administration of President Eduardo Frei against MIR leaders Víctor Toro and his own nephew, Andrés Pascal Allende, be dropped. In addition, he pardoned other MIR members who had been jailed for illegal activities under the previous administration. He ignored the MIR's illegal land seizures, although the MIR killed at least 122 people while accomplishing them. After receiving presidential pardon, MIR cadre Max Joel Marambio was given the job of heading up the 50- to 100-person unauthorized palace guard, Allende's "Group of Personal Friends."

In 1972, the Communist Party sponsored a propaganda campaign against the MIR, accusing it of serving CIA interests. Despite opposition from other leftist parties, 3,000 people attended the MIR's popular assembly that year at the University of Concepción. The MIR's position was that the best way to defend the revolutionary process was to weaken the Allende government and split his Coalición de Unidad Popular (Popular Unity Coalition).

Allende and the Communists fought back by publicly denouncing the leaders of the MIR. One of the few occasions on which Allende directly ordered government forces to fight against the MIR occurred when he was warned that the MIR was about to seize private and state food distribution agencies. On April 4, 1973, the police arrested thirty MIR members and wounded ten as the MIR attempted to carry out this plan.

Following a period of massive inflation and decreasing real wage rates, the Chilean middle class became alienated from the Allende regime, which was subsequently overthrown by a military junta led by army General August Pinochet on September 11, 1973.

The MIR declared war against the military regime. By 1974 most of the MIR's members had gone underground or were dead, with MIR secretary general Miguel Enríquez falling in a gun battle with government troops in Santiago on October 5 of that year. MIR activities were seriously curtailed during the government crackdown. During this period, 123 MIR leaders disappeared. Nevertheless, the MIR refused an offer of truce made by the armed forces' intelligence service on September 10, 1974.

On January 8, 1975, the crackdown continued. Twelve army officers were sentenced to up to fifteen years in prison for collaborating with the MIR. Continued government repression of the leftist opposition led to the deaths of numerous MIR members, causing the MIR to lose much of its power and its ability to seriously jeopardize Pinochet's authoritarian regime.

In November 1975, the government announced that fifteen members of the MIR had been arrested as a result of "Operación Bumerang Rojo" (Red Boomerang Operation), under which the MIR secretly aided the passage of 1,200 extremists into Chile from Argentina's Ejército Revolucionario del Pueblo. Included in the group was exiled MIR secretary general Andrés Pascal Allende, who went into exile in Costa Rica in 1976 but secretly returned to Chile in 1986.

In the late 1970s, MIR guerrillas were involved in hundreds of armed attacks and clashes with government forces. The 1980s brought renewed terrorist activities by the MIR, and bombings increased in Santiago and other cities. In 1984 the MIR established a new guerrilla arm, the Fuerzas Armadas de Resistencia Popular (Popular Resistance Armed Forces). It also continued its campaign against the military government by assassinating a former government intelligence chief in 1980 and a military commander in 1983. One of its leaders, Arturo Villavella, died in combat in 1983.

In 1987 the MIR split into an MIR National Secretariat, which supported Andrés Allende's policy of conducting guerrilla warfare, and a Central Committee, which sought to foster an open relationship with other political parties and eventually joined the political mainstream United Left coalition. Andrés Allende and his followers continued to fight against the military, imperialism, and capitalism even after the end of the military government in 1990. They still seek to establish a true socialist state.

Bibliographical Commentary

Out of the Ashes: Life, Death and Transfiguration of Democracy in Chile, 1933–1988, by James Whelan, is a scholarly, comprehensive treatment of the Chilean reality from 1833 to 1988 and includes numerous references and substantial information about subversive activities. Although *A Nation of*

Enemies: Chile Under Pinochet, by Pamela Constable and Arturo Valenzuela, which focuses mainly on the government of General Augusto Pinochet, does not devote exclusive space to discussion of guerrilla activities, the text frequently touches upon the actions of the groups. In *The Tragedy of Chile,* Robert J. Alexander concentrates on the creation and development of the Movimiento de Izquierda Revolucionaria.

5

COLOMBIA

EJERCITO DE LIBERACION NACIONAL (ELN)
Army of National Liberation

Initiated activities in 1964; operates in northeastern Colombia, in northern and southern Santander, Cauca, Caquetá, and Antioquia, and in the intendancy of Arauca; national-patriotic liberation movement with Marxist and Castrist overtones; maximum estimated strength of 3,100; led by Fabio Vásquez Castaño, Nicolás Bautista, Ricardo Lara Parada, Domingo Lain, Manuel Pérez, Nicolás Rodríguez, and Francisco Galán; plagued by bloody internal struggles; supported by Cuban funds, kidnappings, bank robberies, and other sources; still active.

In the early 1960s, a group of students led by Fabio Vásquez Castaño explored the possibility of starting a guerrilla foco in the department of Santander. Vásquez was neither a peasant nor a member of the Communist Party. His ideological affiliation lay with the Movimiento de Obreros, Estudiantes y Campesinos (MOEC, Movement of Workers, Students and Peasants), Colombia's first revolutionary group. The Ejército de Liberación Nacional, however, was strongly pro-Cuban and stated as its social goal the "conquest of power for the popular classes" (Radu and Tismaneanu 1990: 157).

For the ELN, guerrilla warfare was the indispensable means by which to solve Colombia's problems. Its thrust was mostly rural, though its leaders often talked about the revolutionary potential of student youth, and it was predominantly a student and middle-class movement with strong ties to the University of Santander in Bucaramanga. Many of its militants were trained in Cuba or at home.

The group was constituted on July 4, 1964, and surfaced in the town of Simacota on January 7, 1965, the sixth anniversary of the foundation of the MOEC. Twenty-seven guerrillas entered the town at dawn and held it for two hours, leaving behind a manifesto and five dead policemen. With this action, the guerrillas were trying to show by direct example that armed struggle was not only feasible but also the only road to change in Colombia.

The ELN succeeded in capitalizing on the radical feelings of several Colombian priests. Its most famous recruit was Camilo Torres, a young priest from a distinguished Colombian family who had developed a large following among students and others with his social and political militancy. Torres was killed in February 1966, just a few weeks after joining the ELN.

The ELN at one point was one of the most active groups in Colombia but was eventually weakened by its fanaticism and fierce internal struggles, which were sparked by a bitter debate on who was responsible for the death of Camilo Torres. This infighting resulted in the execution of militants such as Julio Medina Morón and Julio Portocarrero as well as in the defection of many followers. In the late 1960s, Jaime Arenas Reyes, a student guerrilla who had surrendered to the army, charged that guerrilla war had become a "useless sacrifice of students and peasants" (Radu and Tismaneanu 1990: 160). Arena himself was sentenced to death and executed by the ELN. In addition, splits within the organization led on several occasions to the formation of rival guerrilla forces like the Frente Simón Bolívar, established in 1968.

The ELN's leadership and urban network were heavily decimated in 1973 when the army launched an offensive code-named "Operación Anorí." Manuel and Antonio Vásquez Castaño (Fabio's brothers) were killed and Fabio Vásquez left for Cuba. By the end of 1979, the group had been reduced to operating in the middle Magdalena region, mainly in Arauca intendancy and the northeastern region of Caquetá.

The year 1983 saw a revival of the group thanks to a merger between two of the ELN fronts, one led by Nicolás Rodríguez (aka "Gambino"), a peasant guerrilla, and the other by Spanish priest Manuel Pérez. On July 17, ELN commandos occupied the offices of the news agency Agence France Presse in Bogotá and transmitted a communiqué on their objectives. ELN guerrillas also spread their message in the cities through oral propaganda campaigns.

In that same month, the ELN organized three dynamite attacks against U.S.-owned buildings in the city of Bucaramanga to support the struggle of "our Central American brothers against Yankee imperialism" (Radu and Tismaneanu 1990: 159). But its most daring operation came toward the end of the year. On November 22, the ELN kidnapped President Belisario Betancur's brother. The guerrillas released their hostage unharmed on December 7, 1983.

The group's revival was also of an economic nature. The ELN fattened its coffers with kidnapping ransoms paid by Occidental Petroleum as well as with the *vacunas* (shots), periodic payments made by landowners to the guerrillas to ensure that they would not be kidnapped. Though reluctant at first to join the truce talks with the government, the movement decided in early 1984 to participate in negotiations.

Guerrilla activity did not end, however. In 1986, members of the ELN began a strong campaign against multinational oil companies in the eastern plains. Some incursions caused damage estimated at nearly $50 million, and the actions frequently disrupted the flow down the pipeline, which was jointly owned by Occidental, Shell, and Ecopetrol, the Colombian state oil corporation.

In 1988 the guerrillas finally formed an umbrella group, the Coordinadora Guerrillera Simón Bolívar (Simón Bolívar Guerrilla Coordinator), to negotiate democratization with the government. But the ELN, along with the Ejército Popular de Liberación (EPL, Popular Army of Liberation), continued to hedge on a commitment to the new organization. When the constituent assembly was about to meet in early 1991, some 11,000 guerrillas of the Fuerzas Armadas Revolucionarias de Colombia (FARC, Revolutionary Armed Forces of Colombia) and the ELN launched a major series of military actions to protest their exclusion from the political process. During this operation, the insurgents killed twenty-five Colombian police. In one attack, rebels killed twelve members of Colombia's narcotics police in an ambush near the Caribbean coast. In another action, the insurgents killed thirteen police, two security agents, and an army lieutenant and damaged oil pipelines in other parts of the country.

On May 6 of that year, the Coordinadora Guerrillera Simón Bolívar issued a communiqué distributed in the Colombian Constitutional Assembly. In the six-point document, the guerrilla command announced its willingness to meet government delegates at Cravo Norte, a small community 250 miles northeast of Bogotá, to discuss peace. The FARC became the last guerrilla movement dating back to the 1960s to enter into peace negotiations.

Early in 1992, the ELN was carrying out kidnappings (such as that of former minister Argelino Durán) and ambushing the military in Casabe and Valdivia, north of Bogotá, to pressure the government in the peace negotiations. The talks collapsed completely. There is no dialogue at present.

EJERCITO POPULAR DE LIBERACION (EPL)
Popular Army of Liberation

Founded in 1967; operated in the departments of Antioquia and Córdoba, with urban support networks in Bogotá, Medellín, Montería, Bucaramanga, Barrancabermeja, Cali, and Florencia; first Colombian group with Maoist orientation; led by Amanda Ramírez, Rafael Vergara Navarro, Francisco Caraballo, Bernardo Ferreira Grandet, and Jaime Fajardo; supported by Cuba and China; gave up armed struggle in 1984 after negotiations with the government.

The Ejército Popular de Liberación was created in 1967 by the Partido Comunista Colombiano—Marxista Leninista (PCC-ML, Colombian Communist Party—Marxist-Leninist) as its guerrilla arm following peasant revolts in Sinú and San Jorge. The PCC-ML itself originated from a schism with the Partido Comunista Colombiano in 1965.

EPL ranks were made up of peasants, workers, and students. It was the first pro-Chinese group in Latin America to employ the Maoist strategy of revolutionary struggle and apply Mao's ideas to Colombia. It advocated total nationalization and confiscation of all important industrial and agricultural firms, companies, and property. Its message was addressed primarily to peasants, but EPL maintained that the working class had a fundamental role in the revolutionary struggle. It engaged in rural guerrilla warfare, peasant indoctrination, and the development of a popular army.

In the 1960s many peasants joined the movement. Beginning in 1975, however, the EPL limited its operations mainly to urban areas, although it undertook some rural attacks and kidnappings in later years. It advocated a protracted war combined with a terrorist approach. In September 1978, the Movimiento de Autodefensa Obrera (Movement of Labor Self-Defense), the urban branch of the EPL, surfaced in Bogotá, claiming credit for the assassination of former government minister Rafael Pardo. Throughout 1979–1980, the activities of the EPL declined. It was inactive for some months in 1980 and reemerged in 1981.

In May 1982, Belisario Betancur of the Conservative Party won the presidential election and proceeded to negotiate with Congress for an amnesty law for guerrilla groups. Law 35 of 1982, signed on November

20, granted amnesty to all those in armed conflict with the government before that date. Guerrillas already in jail for the pardoned crimes would be released. The EPL denounced Law 35, however, as well as those members of the FARC and the Movimiento 19 de Abril (M-19, April 19th Movement) who accepted it. Later, however, the group announced its decision to adhere to the prevailing tendency toward national reconciliation. It came to an agreement with Betancur's government after negotiations mediated with the help of novelist and Nobel laureate Gabriel García Márquez, and it abandoned armed struggle in 1984.

FUERZAS ARMADAS REVOLUCIONARIAS
DE COLOMBIA (FARC)
Revolutionary Armed Forces of Colombia

Initiated activity in May 1966; operates mainly in the departments of Huila, Caquetá, Tolima, Cauca, Boyacá, Santander, and Antioquia; peasant-based Marxist; maximum strength estimated at between 4,000 and 7,200; led by Pedro Antonio Marín, Manuel Marulanda Vélez, Jacobo Arenas, Jaime Guaraca, Alfonso Cano, and Raúl Reyes; supports itself through drug-traffic operations, kidnappings, and bank robberies; still active in armed struggle.

After the destruction of the autonomous "republic" of Marquetalia, one of several social experiments sponsored by the Partido Comunista Colombiano, party activist Manuel Marulanda Vélez, also known as "Tirofijo" because of his ability as a marksman, announced that he would continue the armed struggle against the government.

At this point, the Liberal and Conservative parties struck an agreement known as the *Frente Nacional* (National Front) in order to put an end to *La Violencia* (The Violence), the political bloodshed between the two parties dating back to 1948. According to the agreement, the two parties would take turns in leading the country, alternating every four years. Although the accord did serve its stated purpose, it also closed off opportunities for other political groups.

Unlike many other Communist parties in the hemisphere, the PCC supported armed struggle and continued to do so well into 1967. On July 20, 1964, a guerrilla assembly called for victory in an agrarian anti-imperialist revolution. On September 30, 1964, the first conference of guerrillas and self-detachments of the south established the Southern Bloc. In less than a year, the Southern Bloc had evolved into the Fuerzas Armadas Revolucionarias de Colombia, the armed branch of the PCC, and in January 1966 the FARC was formally established at the 10th Congress of the Communist Party.

The FARC demanded, among other things, a 50 percent reduction in land and property taxes and a 40 percent reduction in public utility rates, and it advocated nationalization of foreign enterprises. Although the FARC expressed solidarity with the Cuban revolution, it did not follow the Cuban model. After 1967, it grew apart from the Communists and its support from them ended. The backing it had received from workers, students, and radical priests also declined.

For the next twenty years, the group oriented its activity toward rural guerrilla strategy. The FARC was particularly successful in mobilizing peasants in Caquetá, Meta, Santander, and Arauca. The group also organized peasant self-defense detachments in the central Magdalena region.

Changes in the political landscape, however, had an impact on the FARC. Law 35, the amnesty measure spearheaded by Belisario Betancur, was signed on November 20. Betancur also created a Peace Commission to negotiate a definitive peace with the guerrillas.

For its part, in October of that year the FARC proposed a truce in its own peace plan to Betancur. The group asked that a "reform of the political customs of the country" take place between July 20, 1983, and July 20, 1985 (Radu and Tismaneanu 1990: 151). The FARC became divided over the issue of negotiations with the government, however, and continued the struggle in 1983 with attacks on military and civilian targets. In its first 1983 operation, a 120-man column from the group's seventh front attacked the town of Toribio in the Cauca valley. As a result of this infighting, the most extreme FARC guerrillas created the Frente Ricardo Franco in February 1984. FARC leaders referred to these dissidents, who described themselves as part of the FARC, as "common bandits" (Radu and Tismaneanu 1990: 154).

The government pressed on with the concept of an armistice. In April 1984, Marulanda Vélez accepted the truce proposed by Betancur's government and announced his intention to enter politics and run for a seat in Parliament.

In 1985, former FARC members founded a legal party, the Unidad Patriótica (UP, Patriotic Unity), fielding a candidate in the 1986 presidential election and garnering 4.5 percent of the vote. But between 1984 and the end of the decade, the FARC continued to grow in numbers and the violence continued, with only brief truces and periods when FARC leaders showed a willingness to engage in peace talks. The organization's maximum strength was placed at between 4,000 and 7,000 fighters. In addition, numerous press reports and government documents linked the FARC to the cultivation of coca and its production, processing, and commercialization.

Throughout its years of activity, the FARC and its splinter group engaged in the practice of killing militants labeled as "traitors and collaborators." According to a Colombian Army report on 1982 guerrilla activity, the FARC killed thirteen soldiers and ten policemen in ambushes and armed clashes, but it also killed 162 civilians, most of them members of peasant families in the areas of mid-Magdalena, the department of Caquetá, and the eastern plains. And in 1985, following the discovery of 160 bodies in southern Colombia, the Frente Ricardo Franco admitted to ordering the executions on the grounds that the men belonged to military intelligence. The Frente even sentenced to death the chiefs of the FARC hierarchy in November 1986. As late as April 1991, armed forces discovered common graves in La Uribe region in a jungle area near a former FARC camp. The military claimed that these remains (of some 400 persons) belonged to FARC guerrillas executed by their own comrades.

Toward the end of the 1980s, vendettas by drug traffickers against leftists took a severe toll on the UP. More than 1,000 militants were assassinated, including Jaime Pardo, the 1986 presidential candidate.

In December 1990, President César Gavíria ordered an all-out attack on the *Casa Verde* stronghold of the FARC as part of his strategy to induce guerrilla groups still in opposition to give up violent struggle and join the political process. In response, the FARC and the ELN launched their own offensive in January 1991. The insurgents killed twenty-five Colombian police. In one attack, rebels killed twelve members of Colombia's narcotics police in an ambush near the Caribbean coast. In another action, the insurgents killed thirteen police, two security agents, and an army lieutenant and damaged oil pipelines in other parts of the country.

On May 6 of that year, the Coordinadora Guerrillera Simón Bolívar (Simón Bolívar Guerrilla Coordinator), a loose alliance of FARC and ELN elements, issued a communiqué to be distributed in the Colombian Constitutional Assembly. In the six-point document, the guerrilla command announced its willingness to meet government delegates at Cravo Norte, a small community 250 miles northeast of Bogotá, to discuss peace.

The FARC's violent activities, however, did not abate. In 1991 alone, FARC elements carried out 370 kidnappings. Talks between the government and the guerrillas were frequently interrupted, and they eventually broke down. At present there is no dialogue between the FARC and the government, but there is precedent to indicate that talks may revive at some unspecified future date.

MOVIMIENTO DE OBREROS, ESTUDIANTES Y CAMPESINOS (MOEC)
Movement of Workers, Students and Peasants

Founded in January 1959; first revolutionary movement in Colombia; led by Antonio Larrota and Federico Arango; defunct by 1961.

The Movimiento de Obreros, Estudiantes y Campesinos was a revolutionary group associated with dissident elements from the Gaitanist wing of the Liberal Party and the Communist Party. Strongly pro-Cuban, the MOEC attempted to organize guerrilla groups in the department of Cauca, but it disintegrated in May 1961 after Larrota and other leaders were killed.

MOVIMIENTO 19 DE ABRIL (M-19)
April 19th Movement

Founded on March 8, 1974, and active until 1990; operated in the Cauca valley and in Cali, Tolima, and Medellín; embraced a combination of nationalism, socialism, and Guevarism; pro-Cuban; led by Jaime Bateman Cayón, Alvaro Fayad, Iván Marino Ospina, Rosemberg Pabón Pabón, Gustavo Arias, Carlos Pizarro León Gómez, and Antonio Navarro Wolff; most notorious operation was the seizure of the Palace of Justice in 1985; supported by Cuba, Palestine Liberation Organization, and drug connections; at present has become a political party.

The Movimiento 19 de Abril was founded by a group of former Castrist guerrilla fighters frustrated over the failure of the previous organizations, the FARC and the ELN, to take power. Jaime Bateman Cayón had been a member of the Juventud Comunista (Communist Youth) and later of the FARC. The movement defined itself as nationalist and revolutionary and was devoted to prolonged war, popular mass fronts, and armed struggle.

The M-19 originally drew its members from several groups, principally from the socialist side of the political party Alianza Nacional Popular (ANAPO, Popular National Alliance) and, to a lesser extent, from outcast members of the FARC and the Communist Party. The group took its name from the date, April 19, 1970, when ANAPO's ex-president General Gustavo Rojas Pinillas lost the presidential election, allegedly by fraud, to Misael Pastrana Borrero. The group was born at a Bogotá meeting in 1972 but did not engage in its first guerrilla action until January 1974, when it stole a sword and spurs of nineteenth-century independence hero Simón Bolívar from the liberator's home, now a museum. ANAPO quickly renounced any affiliation with the new rebel movement.

The M-19 sought to increase public participation with the goal of political reform and the eventual instigation of a socialist state. Although left-wing and with ties to Cuba, the leaders stressed that it was not a Marxist movement, even though many considered it so. The M-19 has been described as an anti-oligarchic, anti-imperialist, "armed populist" movement. The organization was able to build a strong middle-class constituency in addition to a substantial lower-class base. The M-19 was the first Colombian guerrilla movement to transcend guerrilla warfare in its classic sense by promoting a viable political platform in addition to military action. Its objective was to nationalize the revolution, make it a *pachanga* (celebration). Over the years, the M-19 maintained close connections with Cuba, particularly in the export of drugs, according to various reports. The maximum strength of its cadres has been estimated at more than 2,000.

Between 1974 and 1979, the group worked to project a Robin Hood–type image by distributing food to the poor. A common tactic involved seizing milk trucks and passing the milk out to residents of both rural and urban areas. Although the organization's following was always stronger in the cities, particularly the regions around Cali and Barranquilla, such activities allowed the M-19 to build a broad base of support. On February 15, 1976, the M-19 kidnapped and eventually killed the president of the Colombian Confederation of Workers, José Raquel Mercado, charging him with crimes against the working class. In January of 1979, the guerrillas stole approximately 5,000 weapons from the armed forces arsenal at Cantón Norte.

From February 27 to April 27, 1980, the M-19 occupied the embassy of the Dominican Republic, taking fifty-seven hostages. The ambassadors from the United States, Israel, and Mexico were taken, along with eleven other diplomats and the papal nuncio. The siege ended when the guerrillas left for Cuba with twelve hostages aboard a plane provided by the government of President Julio César Turbay Ayala. The hostages were later freed in Havana. Their demand that the trials of 219 M-19 members be monitored by the Inter-American Human Rights Commission was met.

Chester Allen Bitterman, a U.S. citizen believed to be an operative for the CIA, was kidnapped and killed by the organization in January 1981. As early as March 1981, however, the M-19 began peace negotiations with the government. President Turbay Ayala signed a bill providing amnesty for all guerrillas who laid down their arms within three months. Also at this time, a rift in the M-19 created a faction called the Coordinadora Nacional de Bases (National Coordinator of Bases), composed of more militant members who rejected negotiations. Other acts of compromise included a second presidential offer of amnesty in November 1982 and a truce that led to the release of twenty-five of the M-19's members from prison. The truce ended in April 1983 when the M-19 claimed that President Belisario Betancur could not control the military, which had engaged in violent acts against the M-19 during the cease-fire. On April 28, Bateman Cayón was killed in an air crash. In November, the M-19 entered into an alliance with the FARC and the ELN.

It is widely accepted that the M-19 was involved in coca production and trafficking (as were other insurgency groups), often providing protection to peasant producers and using profits to finance its operations.

On March 14, 1984, M-19 guerrillas undertook a major attack on Florencia prison in Caquetá. In this siege, some 200 guerrillas took 140 hostages and released 158 prisoners. Four civilians, one prison guard, and twenty-six M-19 members died. Rebel leaders, in the midst of peace talks, denounced the attack, declaring it had been led by M-19 exiles. Former M-19 leader Dr. Carlos Toledo Plata, who had been living under terms of amnesty, was assassinated on August 10 by a paramilitary group. The following day, the M-19 responded by occupying the Cali suburb of Yumbo in a joint effort with the FARC. The conflict resulted in the deaths of twelve guerrillas, three policemen, and two civilians; in addition, the guerrillas took eighteen hostages, who were eventually freed. Thirteen days later, a one-year cease-fire agreement was signed despite the fact that several M-19 members were wounded in a police ambush as the delegates approached the ceremony. The M-19 successfully used the cease-fire to promote itself and build political support, although the cease-fire was threatened by the arrests of three M-19 members on charges of arms possession and by combat with the armed forces in December 1984 and January 1985.

In February 1985, Alvaro Fayad replaced Iván Marino Ospina as leader of the movement's congress. In May 1985, following attempted assassinations against several M-19 leaders, the cease-fire ended. The rest of the year was marked by intense violence. Right-wing groups along with the military stepped up their eradication efforts. Iván Marino Ospina was killed in combat August 28, and the M-19 lost territory in the Cauca region. In October, heavy fighting took place in the Cauca valley and the M-19 took heavy casualties. Also that month, the M-19 failed in an assassination of Colombian Army general Rafael Samudio Molina.

On November 6, 1985, the M-19 launched its most sensational operation, and one that backfired completely: It occupied the Palace of Justice in downtown Bogotá. The siege, which involved 400 hostages, was intended to be a mock trial of President Betancur to produce evidence that the military was responsible for the end of the cease-fire. Betancur refused to negotiate with the guerrillas, and at 11:40 A.M. the next day, after the release of 300 hostages, the military stormed the building. The battle that ensued, which involved tanks, rocket launchers, and possibly explosives carried by the M-19, quickly turned the palace into an inferno. Approximately 106 people died in the attack, including eleven hostages and eleven Supreme Court justices. The exact number of guerrilla casualties involved is unknown, although forty-one rebels are believed to have died in the palace.

Crippling to the Betancur administration and a dark stain on the military's effectiveness, the Palace of Justice operation also marked the beginning of the M-19's decline. The rebels now suffered from a lack of direction following the recent deaths of many prominent members, including the loss of five top leaders in the palace siege. Also, because of that episode they lost the popular support they had enjoyed up to that moment. Furthermore, Fayad was killed by police in March 1986, leaving leadership of the M-19 to Carlos Pizarro León Gómez. That month as well, some 300 M-19 guerrillas laid siege to a Cali suburb and were met by strong military opposition, resulting in heavy casualties for the rebels. In July, the M-19 failed in an assassination attempt against Interior Minister Jaime Castro, an assault undertaken in retaliation for the storming of the Palace of Justice.

At this time, the M-19 also conducted joint operations with other dissident movements, including the EPL, the ELN, the Partido Revolucionario de los Trabajadores (Revolutionary Workers' Party), and Patria Libre (Free Homeland), under the umbrella designation of Coordinadora Nacional Guerrillera (National Guerrilla Coordinating Board). It also pursued initiatives beyond the Colombian border with the creation of the Batallón América (America Battalion), which counted among its ranks Peruvians and Ecuadorans and was supposed to be an alliance of Latin American revolutionary elements.

In 1988, conservative leader Alvaro Gómez Hurtado was kidnapped by the M-19. Despite its activity, the movement was weakened, and it entered into peace negotiations with President Virgilio Barco's administration (1986–1990). During this period of inactivity, the rebels continued to conduct kidnappings intended to promote peace, demanding pledges for dialogue from political and religious leaders as ransom, but refrained from undertaking other major endeavors.

The peace process took nearly four years but finally resulted in a pact providing for national dialogue, amnesty, and an end to the M-19's insurgency role. M-19 leaders Pizarro and Navarro Wolff proclaimed armed struggle as obsolete and contrary to the needs of human progress. On March 7 and 8, 1990, members of the movement turned in their arms and entered civilian life. Despite the fact that Pizarro was assassinated soon after the pact was signed, the M-19 has become a powerful force in Colombian politics. In the December 9, 1990, elections, the M-19 Democratic Alliance received about 30 percent of the popular vote in the Constituent Assembly tasked with rewriting the Colombian Constitution. On January 31, 1991, Navarro Wolff returned Bolívar's sword back to its rightful location at Bolívar's home.

Bibliographical Commentary

Despite their notoriety and longevity, Colombia's numerous guerrilla groups generally receive treatment only in large works covering guerrillas throughout Latin America or taking a broad look at Colombian history and politics. Richard Gott's *Guerrilla Movements in Latin America* is an authoritative and detailed source for the older groups, like the Fuerzas Armadas Revolucionarias de Colombia and the Ejército de Liberación Nacional. *Latin American Insurgencies*, by Georges Fauriol, and *Les luttes armées en Amerique Latine*, by Alain Gandolfi, offer objective accounts of the activities of all major movements. *The Making of Modern Colombia*, by David Bushnell, published in 1993, includes carefully researched, up-to-date material, mainly about the Movimiento 19 de

Abril. In his *Guerrillas and Revolution in Latin America: A Comparative Study of Insurgents and Regimes Since 1956*, Timothy Wickham-Crowley approaches the issue mainly from a sociological perspective. *Colombia: Violencia y democracia* and Gonzalo Sánchez G. and Donny Meertens's *Bandoleros, gamonales y campesinos: El caso de la violencia en Colombia* offer insight into the philosophical issues surrounding violence in Colombia. *Colombia Hoy* and contemporary magazines such as *Semana* are useful for cross-referencing information.

6

COSTA RICA

LA FAMILIA
The Family

Active from 1981 to 1983; operated in San José; Marxist-Leninist; led by Miguel Regueira, Mario Guillén García, Alejandra Bonilla, Annette Bonilla, and Freddy Rivera Lizano.

La Familia was the first leftist subversive group to operate in Costa Rica. The group supported the theory of guerra popular prolongada, and its goal was to overthrow the bourgeois state. It engaged in the theft of cars, license plates, and weapons. On March 17, 1981, La Familia placed a bomb at the Honduran Embassy and attacked a group of Marines assigned to the U.S. Embassy. In April 11, the group attempted to set off a bomb at the bust of former President John F. Kennedy in San Pedro de Montes de Doa Square in San José. The plan failed and the group of four escaped after a shootout with police eight days later. On June 12, there was another shootout with police. Three policemen and a taxi driver died in the incident.

Police discovered the group's safe house in Mozotal de Goicoechea on June 17, 1981, and seized its archives as well as documentation and weapons. The main leaders were arrested and condemned to various prison terms in 1983.

ORGANIZACION PATRIOTICA SANTAMARIA/
EJERCITO DE LA DEMOCRACIA Y LA SOBERANIA (OPS)
Santamaría Patriotic Organization/
Army of Democracy and Sovereignty

Active from 1986 to 1988; led by Bolívar Díaz Rojas, Domingo Solís, Ricardo Araya Almanza, Francisco Guier Almanza, German Guendel Angulo, and Livia Cordero Gené.

Information about this group is sketchy. It was created sometime in 1985 by a group of twenty-one Costa Ricans when they contacted the government of Moammar Khadafy to try and turn the Organización Patriótica Santamaría into an affiliate of the Batallón América Libre, an insurgent continent-wide group with ties to the Libyan dictator. Estimates of the OPS's strength vary from 50 to 200 members. The militants are believed to have received military training and funding from Libya.

The group was responsible for three bombings in three consecutive years. On April 17, 1986, and designed on this month to commemorate the U.S. bombing of Tripoli, a bomb went off at the U.S. consulate in San José. On April 27, 1987, a dynamite-based explosive was found near the Centro Cultural Costarricense Norteamericano, a cultural institution. Due to a faulty mechanism, the explosion was small. The third bombing took place on April 19, 1988, also near the Centro Cultural.

On July 22, 1988, the OPS attacked a vehicle from a company called Alpre S.A. that was transporting a payroll for workers on a ranch in the Guanacaste region, and on July 29 the group used the money to finance the robbery of the Banco del Exterior de España in Panama.

According to some accounts, the OPS was connected to other Latin American insurgent groups, such as the Salvadoran guerrillas. Some members of the OPS took part in the 1989 Salvadoran guerrilla offensive, and some were active in the Colombian M-19.

Bibliographical Commentary

Because of their lack of real influence and ideological precision, there is very little material about Costa Rican groups. Georges Fauriol, in *Latin American Insurgencies,* briefly identifies some groups, but the bulk of the information regarding their activities is found in contemporary press accounts.

7

CUBA

MOVIMIENTO 26 DE JULIO (M-26)
July 26th Movement

Active from 1953 to 1959, when it overthrew the government of Fulgencio Batista and gained power; operated in Santiago, Oriente province, Sierra Maestra Mountains, and Havana; inspired by Castrism, a mixture of Cuban nationalism, and Marxism; led by Fidel Castro, Raúl Castro, Ernesto "Che" Guevara, Camilo Cienfuegos, Frank País, Abel Santamaría, David Salvador, Armando Hart, and René Ramos Latour.

On March 10, 1952, three months before elections were to be held in Cuba, Fulgencio Batista took power in a coup d'état. His military dictatorship suspended the constitution, dissolved all political parties, and in general stood for prosperity at the expense of personal freedom. As repression grew under Batista, Fidel Castro, a lawyer and sometime member of the Partido Revolucionario Ortodoxo (Revolutionary Orthodox Party), which stood for the end of government corruption, circulated a petition denouncing the illegitimacy of the Batista regime.

On March 24, 1952, Castro filed a brief before the Court of Constitutional Guarantees calling for Batista's arrest. The Cuban court ruled against the motion, which represented the first step in Castro's long road to seize control of Cuba.

Castro recruited people for a campaign against Batista. Hoping to spur a mass uprising, on July 26, 1953, 170 guerrillas attacked the Moncada barracks in Santiago de Cuba. Fidel Castro and his brother Raúl led the attacks, and the weapons were paid for by the rebels themselves. The attack failed miserably, and Castro's right-hand man up to that point, Abel Santamaría, was tortured and killed by the Batista forces. The remaining rebels (including Raúl and Fidel) were captured a week later, and Fidel Castro was sentenced to fifteen years in a prison on the Isle of Pines.

In his book *La historia me absolverá,* based on his trial defense, Castro accused the corrupt regime of usurpation of power and of creating social injustice and causing social misery for Cubans. He also called for a land reform and a variety of social programs as well as for a society free of foreign influence. These basic tenets provided a foundation for the Movimiento 26 de Julio.

Although after coming to power Fidel Castro proclaimed he had always been a Marxist-Leninist, there is no firm evidence to support the position that his movement had a clear leftist agenda from the outset. Rather, he was greatly influenced by the democratic liberal ideas of the university and nineteenth-century patriot José Martí.

Fidel Castro was released from the penitentiary in May 1955 after the government granted a general amnesty. Thus began the second phase of the M-26. Soon after his release, Castro left for Mexico to recruit a guerrilla force and train for his proposed revolution, promising to return and liberate Cuba. Using as a base the house of Cuban exile María Antonia, the rebels were trained by Cuban-born Alberto Bayo, a former officer of the Spanish Republican Army. In September 1956, José Antonio Echeverría, head of the activist movement Directorio Revolucionario (DR, Revolutionary Directorate), went to Mexico and signed a joint action accord with Fidel Castro.

In Mexico, Castro also met with Ernesto "Che" Guevara, an Argentine revolutionary who agreed to join the expedition as a physician. Finally, on November 26, 1956, the revolutionaries set sail back to Cuba on a boat called the *Granma.* The eighty-one men landed in the province of Oriente on December 2, two days after the expected rendezvous date. The scheduled uprisings in Santiago and Manzanillo, of which the Batista government had prior knowledge, were put down before Castro and the *Granma* arrived. Fidel Castro and about twenty of the guerrillas escaped to the Sierra Maestra as Batista circulated erroneous news reports that Castro had been killed and the revolution crushed. On January 17, 1957, the rebels attacked the barracks at La Plata. Following this event, the revolution continued to grow in the Sierra region. While the guerrillas were hiding there, the Auténticos, a rival political party that had spawned the Ortodoxos, was plotting to oust Batista and seize power, all the while expressing support for Castro's uprising.

In addition, members of the Directorio Revolucionario attacked the presidential palace on March 13, 1957, but suffered heavy casualties at the hands of Batista's guards. The Fidelistas expressed solidarity with the DR after the fact, but the two groups had traditionally been rivals.

As the M-26 grew more popular back in Cuba, the Partido Socialista Popular (PSP, Socialist Popular Party), the Cuban Communist Party, which had condemned the original Castro putsch attempt, moved to open a dialogue with Castro and his men. The PSP also provided some support for Castro's forces in the Sierra Maestra, although discrepancies exist as to the extent of its assistance. Some say that the PSP was solely concerned with maintaining the integrity of its own party. However, the Communists stated in 1959 that they had supported the insurrection at the time of the *Granma* landing. The turning point in the relations between Castro's group and the PSP occurred in 1958, when Carlos Rafael Rodríguez visited Castro in the Sierra Maestra and joined forces with the movement.

The urban branch of the M-26 was very active in Santiago and Havana, rallying support for the cause and committing acts of sabotage. In July 1957, Frank País, the main leader of the urban movement, was killed in Santiago. Following his death, the branch continued activities, but it was gradually overshadowed by Castro's rural fighting force. A general strike was called for in April 1958, but it received broad support only in Oriente province.

The movement's most important guerrilla action occurred on December 24, 1958, when "Che" Guevara and his guerrillas took Santa Clara, the capital of Las Villas province, and were then joined up by Camilo Cienfuegos and his forces. On December 27, General Eulogio Cantillo, head of the Cuban Army's troops in the battlefield, proposed talks with the rebels to end the civil war. Cantillo's real motive was to take over control of the government. Batista fled Cuba on the night of December 31, 1958, and Fidel was alerted to Cantillo's plan. Raúl Castro and his force entered Santiago on January 2, 1959. The troops of Cienfuegos and Guevara entered Havana on January 5, and the military rebellion phase of the movement was concluded. The M-26 appointed Manuel Urrutia as the new president, and Fidel Castro became prime minister, replacing Urrutia, on February 16. After taking office, Castro called for yet another strike in order to allow the workers to increase their involvement in the revolution.

It is difficult to pinpoint the exact ending date of the M-26. In late 1959, with the revolution effectively over, Fidel Castro chose not to adapt its administrative structure to better suit the postrevolutionary period, when a new government would be formed. In the final analysis, Fidel Castro was the only real mainstay of the movement, and the decision to continue with the struggle was his alone. To Castro, the M-26 symbolized the rebirth of Cuba. He attempted in 1959 to consolidate all the revolutionary groups under the banner of M-26-7 (his force in the mountains and its civilian allies in the city), but the divisions were too great to form a substantial coalition governing party and eventually Castro took complete control of the M-26-7. Ultimately, Fidel Castro embraced the politics, and military and economic aid, of the Soviet Union.

Bibliographical Commentary

The saga of Fidel Castro has been so exhaustively covered from every conceivable viewpoint that the issue here becomes one of excess of information. K. S. Karol, in *Guerrillas in Power: The Course of the Cuban Revolution*, provides a chronological account of the Cuban political context and the relationship between the Communists and the July 26th Movement. *The Cuba Reader: The Making of a Revolutionary Society*, edited by Philip Brenner, William M. LeoGrande, Donna Rich, and Daniel Siegel, contains a translation of the program manifesto of the July 26th Movement. Finally, Sheldon B. Liss, in *Roots of Revolution: Radical Thought in Cuba*, offers clarification of Fidel Castro's ideological agenda.

8

DOMINICAN REPUBLIC

MOVIMIENTO 14 DE JUNIO (M-14)
June 14th Movement

Operated from the end of the 1950s as a political organization; took up armed struggle November and December 1963, and again in 1970; Marxist-Castrist; led by Manuel Tavárez Justo, Leandro Guzmán, Pedro Bonilla, Juan Miguel Román, Polo Rodríguez, Roberto Duvergé, Juan Mejía.

On September 25, 1963, with the encouragement of the United States, the Dominican army ousted constitutionally elected President Juan Bosch, and replaced him with a junta.

Soon after the coup, which had been staged just seven months after Bosch had taken office, some 250 guerrillas began roaming the Dominican hills and waging a campaign of bombings and countryside ambushes.

These rebels, who were supported by Havana, belonged to the Agrupación 14 de Junio (June 14th Group), named after the date in 1959 of the second, unsuccessful attempt to overthrow Rafael Trujillo, the longtime Dominican Republic dictator who governed from 1930 till May 30, 1961, when he was murdered by a group of soldiers and civilians with CIA backing.

The Movimiento 14 de Junio began initially as a political organization with a nationalist ideology, but the leftist radicalized faction, led by Manuel Tavárez Justo, had gained the central spotlight by mid-1962. At a rally June 14, at a time when the political situation in the Dominican Republic was unstable, Tavárez made an impassioned warning about going to the mountains to take up the armed struggle if there was no other alternative to reform.

The movement split in November 1962, with the more radical faction taking the name Agrupación Política 14 de Junio and the other, more moderate faction, calling itself Partido 14 de Junio (June 14th Party). The more radical faction, with Tavárez at the helm, advocated a revolutionary agenda which included agrarian reform and expropriation. After the overthrow of Bosch, the Agrupación Política 14 de Junio was declared illegal and preparations for armed struggle began in earnest, even though the group had already been taking secret steps toward violent insurrection.

Emilio de los Santos, chief of the ruling junta, advocated a conciliatory approach to dealing with the rebels, but he was outvoted in favor of all out offensive.

Six guerrilla fronts were created in November 1963. One by one all fell. The group was ready to surrender in the last days of December 1963, and it was virtually annihilated when the Dominican armed forces moved in on a gathering of guerrillas at a sawmill near the town of San José de las Matas in the central mountains. When the incident was over, Tavárez was dead, along with fourteen of his comrades. Four guerrillas were captured. The official report said that there had been a shootout. According to other versions, the guerrillas turned themselves in and were killed by the security forces.

Among the dead was Antonio Barreiro, godson of junta chief de los Santos. De los Santos resigned upon hearing the news.

After this unsuccessful episode, many members of the movement were jailed or went into exile.

In 1965, however, elements of the M-14 movement backed leftist colonel Francisco Caamaño Deñó in defending Santo Domingo against the U.S. invasion. Caamaño Deñó was exiled to London after the withdrawal of U.S. troops. From there, he left for Cuba in 1967 to begin preparations for an invasion of the Dominican Republic by leftist forces. When he landed at Caracoles in February 1973, his group consisted of only 9 men, including Caamaño Deñó himself. The entire expedition was killed by government forces within a couple of weeks.

Bibliographical Commentary

Movimiento 14 de Junio: Historia y Documentos, by Tony Raful, is an invaluable source of information on the Dominican guerrilla movement.

English-language sources, however, are scarce. Donald Hodges' *The Latin American Revolution: Politics and Strategy from Apro-Marxism to Guevarism* touches upon the development of the movement, and the *Diction-*

ary of Contemporary Politics of Central America and the Caribbean, edited by Phil Gunson, Greg Chamberlain, and Andres Thompson, can be consulted for general historical background.

9

ECUADOR

¡ALFARO VIVE, CARAJO! (AVC)
Alfaro Lives, Damn It!

Active from 1981 to 1992; operated in Quito, Guayaquil, and Cuenca; its ideology was never clearly defined, but in general it embraced the Pan-American visions of Simón Bolívar and Eloy Alfaro, leftist nationalism, the Marxist-Leninist transformation of Latin America, and the foco theory; led by Ricardo Arturo Jarrín, Juan Carlos Acosta Coloma, Fausto Basantes, Hamed Vazconez, Edgar Frías, Ricardo Merino, and Santiago Kigman; supported itself with bank robberies and kidnappings.

¡Alfaro Vive, Carajo!, which took its name from national independence hero Eloy Alfaro, coalesced gradually beginning in 1981 with elements from various leftist organizations, such as the Movimiento de Izquierda Revolucionaria (MIR, Movement of the Revolutionary Left), the Movimiento Revolucionario de los Trabajadores (MRT, Revolutionary Workers' Movement) and the Movimiento de Izquierda Cristiana (MIC, Christian Left Movement).

The group, pro-Cuban and pro-Sandinista, was composed mostly of middle-class and upper-class youths and intellectuals with ties to universities, although some peasant leaders eventually joined as well. Most of its cadres trained in the Cauca area of Colombia or in Nicaragua, Cuba, the Soviet Union, or Libya.

Fundamentally urban in nature, AVC sought to take power through armed struggle. Its ideology was outlined in a document called *Mientras haya que hacer, nada hemos hecho* (As long as there is something left to do, we have done nothing), which was drawn up at the organization's first annual leadership conference in 1983.

Despite this document, however, Alfaro Vive had no clear-cut ideological content. It described itself as anti-imperialist and anti-oligarchical but attempted to transcend dogma. As a result, the group suffered from internal conflicts and a lack of a distinct direction. For instance, the group's program of action called for political work, but that aspect was overshadowed as the emphasis increasingly shifted to a militaristic approach and spectacular effects.

The group surfaced in 1983 with a press conference. Its first main action was the theft of the bust and sword of Eloy Alfaro. To this day they remain lost because only leaders who were killed in action knew their hiding place.

Alfaro Vive obtained funds mainly through bank robberies and kidnappings. The latter were generally accompanied by requests to have statements published or broadcast. The kidnapping of wealthy banker Naín Isaías Barquet in July 1985 proved to be the beginning of the end for Alfaro Vive. The government of León Febres Cordero refused to negotiate with the guerrillas and instead, in August, ordered an attack on the place where the banker was being held. More than half a dozen people died in the clash that ensued, including Isaías Barquet and guerrilla Juan Acosta Coloma, the son of Francisco Acosta Yepes, president of the Supreme Court of Ecuador. Two Baquerizo Ayala siblings were arrested in Guayaquil in December of the following year in connection with this episode.

The year 1986 was even more catastrophic. Leader Ricardo Merino died in June, Hamed Vazconez fell in September, and Arturo Jarrín in October. Jarrín was arrested in Panama and did not make it back to Ecuador alive. The official version was that he was killed in an armed clash, but other versions point to an execution by the Panamanian or Ecuadoran police.

Another disastrous venture was the group's participation in the Batallón América that the Colombian Movimiento 19 de Abril (M-19) was trying to put together with elements from various Latin American nations. The Batallón América never got off the ground in terms of numerical strength and dissolved when the M-19, its main driving force, began to consider abandoning armed struggle.

Although the group went on to carry out takeovers of radio stations, such as those of El Sol and Musical in Quito in December 1986, the movement never recovered from the setbacks.

In 1987 Santiago Kigman assumed the leadership of the movement, which was now reduced from some 300 armed cadres to about 200, and the idea of giving up the armed struggle began to take root. The organization was never successful in garnering widespread popular support. Its attempts to create popular militias was a complete failure, although some 5,000 people did show up in May 1987 for an Alfaro Vive public demonstration in Quito.

In addition to the decimation of forces and lack of popular support, Alfaro Vive faced other difficulties. The international context was no longer as receptive to armed revolutionary fight as it had been in the past, and the Colombian Movimiento 19 de Abril, with whom Alfaro Vive had connections, had become a legal organization. The approaching end of the Cold War also contributed to the decline of guerrilla struggle.

On February 28, 1991, the guerrillas lay down their weapons after joining into negotiations with the government of President Rodrigo Borja. The group remained active until 1992 with nonclandestine militancy, and at present it is trying to establish itself as a bona fide political party.

Bibliographical Commentary

There is very little scholarly treatment of ¡Alfaro Vive, Carajo! Michael Radu and Vladimir Tismaneanu, in *Latin American Revolutionaries: Groups, Goals, Methods,* offer an overview of the movement. Contemporary press reports are spotty but occasionally provide useful information.

10

EL SALVADOR

EJERCITO REVOLUCIONARIO DEL PUEBLO (ERP)
People's Revolutionary Army

Active from 1972 to 1992, with a protohistory from 1970 to 1972; operated in the departments of Morazán, La Unión, San Vicente, San Miguel, and San Salvador, with reportedly some activity in Honduras; initially Maoist, then increasingly influenced by Nicaragua and Cuba; led by Roque Dalton García, Sebastián Urquilla, Carlos Humberto Portillo, Joaquín Villalobos Hueso, Ana María Guadalupe Martínez, Mercedes del Carmen Letona, and Arquímedes Canadas; supported by Cuba, the Soviet Union, and Nicaragua as well as by kidnappings, bank robberies, the Basque revolutionary organization Euzkadi ta Azkatasuna (ETA), and "war taxes"; represented by the open activities of the front organization Ligas Populares 28 de Febrero (Popular Leagues February 28th) and the Partido de la Revolución Salvadoreña (Party of the Salvadoran Revolution).

The Ejército Revolucionario del Pueblo was established gradually beginning in 1970 by dissident elements of the Juventud Comunista (Communist Youth), radicalized members of the Salvadoran branch of Christian Democratic youth, and members of the Acción Cristiana (Christian Action) group. It was initially known as El Grupo (The Group) and was reportedly involved in some of the first major terrorist operations in El Salvador in 1970, such as the kidnapping and death of Ernesto Regalado Dueñas, scion of a wealthy Salvadoran family.

In 1972 El Grupo evolved into the ERP, a middle-class, ultraradical organization with an unusually large number of women in its ranks. The largest guerrilla organization in El Salvador since 1983, and the most consistently violence-oriented of all Salvadoran insurgent movements, the ERP has had links with Nicaragua's Frente Sandinista de Liberación Nacional (FSLN, Sandinista National Liberation Front) and Guatemala's Ejército Guerrillero de los Pobres (EGP, Guerrilla Army of the Poor). The

main psychological characteristic of its approach to revolutionary violence was *triunfalismo* (triumphant attitude)—the perception that victory
is within immediate reach and that only a last effort, regardless of the
cost, is needed to reach it. Military action, not so much the political aspect of the struggle, was what mattered. From its inception, the ERP engaged in urban terrorism based on the Southern Cone model. *Foquismo*
was also part of its strategy.

In May 1975, following a serious internal dispute over the ERP's tactical approach to the struggle, a dissident faction headed by poet Roque
Dalton split off to form the Fuerzas Armadas de Resistencia Nacional
(FARN, Armed Forces of National Resistance). Extremist leaders who
were subsequently expelled from the ERP murdered Dalton on May 10,
1975. Armando "Pancho" Arteaga was also killed with Dalton. In 1977,
another shakedown occurred at the First Congress of the Partido de la
Revolución Salvadoreña (Party of the Salvadoran Revolution), created
the year before to offset the organization's militaristic image, when the
founder and main leader of the ERP, Sebastián Urquilla, was purged.
The victors of that internal clash, led by Joaquín Villalobos, remained in
control of the group until the culmination of the peace negotiations between the group and the government.

On January 27, 1977, one month before the rigged elections that
brought General Carlos Humberto Romero to power, the ERP kidnapped
Roberto Poma, president of the National Tourism Institute. In answer to
the kidnappers' demands, two guerrillas were freed and a ransom was
paid. But Poma had been wounded during the kidnapping and died
while still in captivity.

The ERP's above ground activities of the front organization, the Ligas
Populares 28 de Febrero, was created by ERP sympathizers within the
National University in February 1978. It had about 10,000 members, including the leaders of some minor unions and student organizations, and
was considered to have the least well-developed political program of all
legal front organizations in El Salvador. This group resorted mostly to
such actions as the occupation of embassies, ministries, farms, and the
like, choosing its tactics with little consideration of outcomes. It was formally disbanded toward the end of 1980.

After October 1979, the ERP's ranking members believed that the
masses were radicalized enough to support an insurrection based on the
Nicaraguan model, but their efforts to create an insurrection in San Salvador failed. After the killing of Dalton, the ERP became a pariah among

the other groups and only returned to join the other organizations with the formation of the Directorio Revolucionario Unificado (DRU, Unified Revolutionary Directorate) on May 22, 1980.

In January 1981, just days before the inauguration of President Ronald Reagan, the ERP managed to attract Cuban and Nicaraguan support for a new bid at insurrection. The group was at the forefront of the final offensive, which eventually failed.

The years 1980–1981 saw an exodus into the countryside by ERP cadres following the government crackdown on guerrilla activities in the cities, but the organization returned to insurrectional tactics in 1982. Militarily the most effective guerrilla group in El Salvador, with a maximum strength estimated at 2,000, by the end of 1986 the ERP probably controlled as many as half of the total fighters in the Frente Farabundo Martí de Liberación Nacional (FMLN, Farabundo Martí National Liberation Front), a five-group coalition of Salvadoran guerrilla groups created in 1982. The ERP was not only efficient on the battlefield but also had a remarkable propaganda network, with its main instrument being Radio Venceremos.

FRENTE FARABUNDO MARTI
DE LIBERACION NACIONAL (FMLN)
Farabundo Martí National Liberation Front

Created in October 1980; operated north and east of Rio Lempa in the departments of Chalatenango, Cabanas, Morazán, Cuscatlán, San Vicente, and Usulután; Marxist-Leninist; led by Salvador Cayetano Carpio, Salvador Sánchez Cerén, and Mélida Anaya Montes (aka "Ana María") (Fuerzas Populares de Liberación—Farabundo Martí—FPL, Popular Forces of Liberation—Farabundo Martí), Ana María Guadalupe Martínez and Joaquín Villalobos Hueso (Ejército Revolucionario del Pueblo—ERP, People's Revolutionary Army), Eduardo Sancho (Fuerzas Armadas de Resistencia Nacional—FARN, Armed Forces of National Resistance), Francisco Jovel (Partido Revolucionario de Trabajadores de Centroamérica—PRTC, Revolutionary Party of the Workers of Central America), and Shafik Jorge Handal (Fuerzas Armadas de Liberación—FAL, Armed Forces of Liberation); supported by the World Front, Nicaragua, Cuba, and the Eastern bloc; received political backing from the Committee in Solidarity with the People of El Salvador (CISPES); maximum strength estimated at 12,000 in 1983; represented by the legal Frente Democrático Revolucionario (FDR, Revolutionary Democratic Front), a collection of predominantly peaceful organizations of which the FMLN was the guerrilla arm; ended armed struggle in 1992.

The Frente Farabundo Martí de Liberación Nacional took its name from Agustín Farabundo Martí, a Communist leader shot before a firing squad in the infamous 1932 massacre, one of the most somber episodes in Salvadoran history. Clashes between peasants and the oligarchy over the country's growing land shortage and subsequent need for economic and social reform had been fairly frequent. In December 1931, a group of army officers had ousted President Alberto Araujo and put General Maximiliano Hernández Martínez into power. Although the junta allowed the Communist Party to participate in the 1932 municipal elections, it later refused to certify its wins. Peasants and workers decided to launch an insurrection, but word on the planned revolt leaked out and leaders were arrested on January 18. Fighting broke out on January 22 and raged on for several days. By the time the armed forces were through, they had killed or executed some 30,000 people, about 2 percent of the total population of the country.

This episode, called the *Matanza* (the Killing), and the subsequent repression kept this segment of society silent until the 1960s and 1970s, when the labor movement and the political opposition rallied. Following the 1972 presidential election, winner José Napoleón Duarte Fuentes of the Partido Demócrata Cristiano (PDC, Christian Democratic Party) was forced into exile by the military, who refused to recognize his victory. Colonel Arturo Molina, the official candidate, took power.

The obvious corruption of the Salvadoran political system led to the emergence of Marxist guerrilla organizations. These operated individually for several years until they eventually joined forces. In May 1980, the leaders of four Salvadoran guerrilla groups—Fuerzas Populares de Liberación (FPL), Ejército Revolucionario del Pueblo (ERP), Fuerzas Armadas de Liberación (FAL), and Fuerzas Armadas de Resistencia Nacional (FARN)—united to form the Directorio Revolucionario Unificado (DRU) to coordinate operations and support efforts. The Partido Revolucionario de Trabajadores de Centroamérica (PRTC) joined later. The DRU became the FMLN in October of that year when the command structures were unified. All factions of the FMLN generally abided by a power structure based on distinctions among groups. The highest body of the organization was the General Command, composed of the top commander from each of the five member organizations. The DRU was made up of three representatives from each group and was widely considered responsible for the majority of the decision making.

The FMLN divided Salvadoran territory into four guerrilla fronts. The Ama Feliciano Western Front encompassed the departments of Santa Ana, Ahuachapán, and Sonsonate. The Modesto Ramírez Central Front was composed of the departments of Chalatenango, San Salvador, La Libertad, and Cuscatlán. The Anastasio Aquino Paracentral Front encompassed the departments of La Paz, San Vicente, and Cabanas. The Francisco Sánchez Western Front included Usulután, San Miguel, Morazán, and La Unión. At this level, the guerrillas were organized into battalions with as many as 300 people, which subsequently were divided into detachments, platoons, and finally squads of as few as eight people. At all levels, women, such as Comandante "Ana María" (Mélida Anaya Montes) of the FPL, actively participated as both soldiers and leaders.

Although elements of the Catholic Church and popular organizations with similar demands supported the FMLN's cause, for actual equipping and training of its forces the organization depended heavily on outside sources. The World Front in Solidarity with the People of El Salvador, founded in 1982, acted in more than forty-two member countries to raise funds for the guerrillas and generate support for them and opposition against the Salvadoran government. In the United States, the Committee in Solidarity with the People of El Salvador openly provided support. Havana and Nicaragua's Sandinista government provided significant amounts of vital weaponry and military training to the FMLN.

The military philosophy of the FMLN was summed up in the belief that nonviolence was useless in bringing about change. The rural poor generally shared this view. It was among them that the FMLN recruited most heavily, and the guerrillas came to depend on the cooperation of the civilian population.

In its first major military move, however, the FMLN made a crucial mistake by vastly overestimating the strength of this support. In January 1981 it attempted the Final Offensive. Leaders envisioned spontaneous popular uprisings in the cities where the guerrillas had done political work, but the mass insurgency never occurred. The FMLN also made serious strategic errors throughout the planning process, overestimating the dissatisfaction with the junta government, the experience of its fighting cadres, and the efficiency of its weaponry supply. Feeling it was necessary to take advantage of the U.S. election before the transition of power led to a further increase in U.S. intervention in El Salvador, the FMLN launched the operation on January 10. At first it seemed the guerrillas were well on the way to victory. San Francisco Gotera, the provincial capital of Morazán, fell, as well as the city of Metapán in the department of Santa Ana. In Santa Ana, the garrison revolted and the installations of the Salvadoran air force were attacked. But by the end of the month, the tide had begun to turn. San Francisco Gotera was abandoned after eight days, and a tactical retreat was ordered. Because of weakness in their urban infrastructure, the guerrillas were unable to bring the offensive to San Salvador.

Although the FMLN failed in its overall objective, it did gain international recognition as a meaningful political and military force. The offensive also helped the guerrillas establish military "zones of control" in rural northern and eastern regions, a key one being the department of Chalatenango.

The year 1982 was crucial for the coordination and organization of factions within the FMLN. After being defeated by the army in another early-year offensive, the guerrilla groups realized the importance of logistical coordination. The factions engaged in a serious effort to iron out policy disputes and overcome their strategical, logistical, and communications problems. The mysterious suicide and murder, respectively, of FPL leaders Salvador Carpio and "Ana María" Montes may have facilitated the internal accord by weakening the FPL's influence over the FMLN. In their stead, ERP theoretician Joaquín Villalobos, and his cooperative policies, became the most powerful influence on the movement.

By 1983, the guerrilla organization was once again on the offensive, escalating the intensity of combat. The ranks swelled with new recruits—an estimated 12,000 people, the largest number ever, could be counted in the guerrilla ranks that year. At this size, the army had only a four-to-one advantage over the guerrillas and realized the new and significant threat the FMLN posed to the government. Backed by increased military aid from the United States, the army felt that a final, decisive victory over the guerrillas was both necessary and easily possible. The FMLN resisted the onslaught by adapting its strategy from a focus on concentrated zones of control to more classic guerrilla-style warfare made up of a campaign of widespread but irregular military actions.

During this time the FMLN also started sabotaging Salvador's economic and transportation systems to counteract U.S. efforts to stabilize what the FMLN called the government's "economy of war" and simultaneously tied up an important number of army troops with having to guard tunnels, bridges, and other fixed structures.

In 1984, President Duarte attempted to end the five-year stalemate between the army and the guerrillas by initiating the first-ever peace talks with the FMLN. These talks failed, however, because of Duarte's inability to control the military. Despite his efforts, the situation remained basically unchanged.

As the standoff in what became a low-intensity conflict continued, support for the guerrillas diminished among a population weary of violence and the sustained counterinsurgency efforts of the military. By 1986, the ranks of the FMLN had dwindled to as few as 5,000 people. In view of these circumstances, FMLN leaders reached the consensus that a complete military victory would be impossible and that an end to the hostilities would necessarily involve at least minimal negotiation with the government. This realization made the FMLN adopt a number of steps. In 1988, Villalobos and Sánchez Cerén traveled to Latin America to seek diplomatic support for their cause. The FMLN also launched a strategic counteroffensive, a program combining a large-scale political action component with military operations, in January 1989. The organization's · successful political initiatives were often cited during this period as proof that no stalemate existed and that the guerrillas' political victory gave them the strategic advantage over the army. In the political arena, through its popular mass organizations, the FMLN had links to the political coalition Frente Democrático Revolucionario.

As part of its new orientation, the FMLN vowed to recognize the results of the 1989 presidential election. The guerrillas supported candidate Guillermo Manuel Ungo Revelo. He was overwhelmingly beaten, however, by both winner Alfredo Cristiani Burkard of the Alianza Republicana Nacionalista (ARENA, Nationalist Republican Alliance) and runner-up Fidel Chávez Mena of the Partido Demócrata Cristiano. Ungo's defeat seemed to refocus the FMLN once again on a military, rather than a political, path. In October of that year the FMLN broke off political negotiations with the ARENA government in response to the bombing of a union headquarters that killed ten of its members.

On November 11, 1989, the FMLN launched yet another offensive. Until this time, the guerrillas had been known as the rural "poor people's army," notoriously lacking networking or support in the cities. But throughout the late 1980s, the FMLN had quietly been building and solidifying urban strongholds. The simultaneous uprisings in cities all over Salvador highlighted the army's shortcomings and its general inability to combat urban insurgency. The army was forced to resort to aerial bombing of the areas where guerrillas held positions. Although this extreme action temporarily defeated the FMLN, the guerrillas still counted the offensive a significant victory because it proved their ability to wage war in both country and city with equal effectiveness.

A bloody incident shortly thereafter further exacerbated hostilities and shocked world public opinion: Six Jesuit priests thought to be supporters and contacts of the FMLN as well as their housekeeper and her young daughter were murdered by a hit squad made up of members of the armed forces. Pressured by the scandalized outcry, President Cristiani asked the United Nations to step in and negotiate for an end to the now escalating conflict.

In January 1990, guerrilla leaders indicated that they would accept UN mediation and resume negotiations. Between November and December of that year, however, the FMLN launched a series of attacks that cost some 300 lives. On New Year's Eve, 1991, a peace treaty brokered by the United Nations was signed between Cristiani's government and the FMLN. The accords provided for a cease-fire and large-scale economic and social reforms, including the FMLN's entry into the Salvadoran political process.

The accord also stipulated a drastic military overhaul involving the dissolution of guerrilla groups as well as of government military and security units, a reduction in the size of the army, and the formation of a national civil police force that all former combatants, both government and guerrilla, would be eligible to join.

FUERZAS ARMADAS DE LIBERACION (FAL)
Armed Forces of Liberation

Active from 1977 to 1992; operated in San Salvador and in the eastern and southeastern regions of the country; orthodox Marxist-Leninist; numbered some 500 fighters plus an estimated 1,500 sympathizers and supporters; led by Abel and Max Cuenca, Shafik Jorge Handal, and Rigoberto López; supported by the USSR; represented by the legal front organizations Partido de Acción Renovadora (Party of Renewal Action), Unión Democrática Nacionalista (Nationalist Democratic Union) and Unión Nacionalista Opositora (Opposing National Union).

The Partido Comunista de El Salvador (PCES, Communist Party of El Salvador) was formally established in 1929, although Communist groups had been active in El Salvador since 1925. The PCES backed the winner of the 1930 elections, Arturo Araujo, but eventually began concentrating its energies in organizing peasants into unions. Following the overthrow of Araujo by General Maximiliano Hernández Martínez and the bloody episode known as La Matanza, in which an estimated 30,000 people were killed during the repression of a popular uprising, the party was virtually destroyed until its reestablishment in 1944.

In addition to focusing on labor issues, the PCES began to develop an electoral strategy. To that end, it formed the Unión Democrática Nacionalista (UDN, Nationalist Democratic Union) in 1969. It joined the Partido Demócrata Cristiano (PDC, Christian Democratic Party) and the Movimiento de Liberación Nacional (Movement of National Liberation) as part of the Unión Nacional Opositora (UNO), a coalition of the Christian and Social Democrats and the Nationalist Democratic Union, in the presidential elections of 1972 and 1977.

Although the UDN participated in the government of the first junta— which lasted until January 1980—following the October 1979 coup, the PCES had been gradually drifting away from the electoral route and toward an alliance with rebel groups engaged in armed struggle. Initially the PCES had eschewed violence as a course of action, a position that had led to the departure of then secretary general Salvador Cayetano Carpio and the foundation of the Fuerzas Populares de Liberación. However, at the 7th Party Congress in April 1977, the PCES decided to take up arms. Toward the end of 1979, the militias that had begun forming in 1977 coalesced as the Fuerzas Armadas de Liberación, with the general secretary of the PCES as its formal commander.

Although one of the last guerrilla movements to come to life in El Salvador, and one of the smallest, the FAL was relatively effective, primarily because of the superior discipline of its recruits and the access to training abroad (in the former USSR, the former East Germany, Bulgaria, Cuba, and Nicaragua).

In 1986, the army launched Operation Phoenix at the Guazapa volcano war front with the intention of dislodging the guerrillas from the area and pushing them to the Honduran border to be crushed. At the height of Phoenix, the FAL evacuated all civilians and nonessential personnel, leaving some fifty combatants. The offensive lasted nearly a year, but the guerrillas held. In Guazapa, they numbered a maximum of 150 fighters.

Shafik Handal, whose faction took over after Carpio split to form the FPL, openly advocated the indiscriminate mining of civilian-inhabited areas and the exploitation of a civilian presence to shield urban guerrilla field operations. Because of this policy, public support for FAL steadily decreased after 1976.

In 1980, the FAL joined the Fuerzas Populares de Liberación, the Ejército Revolucionario del Pueblo, and the Fuerzas Armadas de Resistencia Nacional to form the Frente Farabundo Martí de Liberación Nacional.

FUERZAS ARMADAS DE RESISTENCIA NACIONAL (FARN)
Armed Forces of National Resistance

Active from 1975 to 1992; operated in the departments of Cuscatlán, Usulután, and San Salvador, with some activity in Honduras and Mexico; unorthodox Marxist, with ties to the Catholic Church and the middle class; led by Ernesto Jovel Funes, Augusto Coto, Fermán Cienfuegos, and Anabel Ramos; represented legally by the Partido de Resistencia Nacional (PRN, National Resistance Party) and the Frente de Acción Popular Unido (FAPU, United Front of Popular Action).

Organized by dissident ERP members, the Fuerzas Armadas de Resistencia Nacional was the most visible of Salvadoran terrorist groups because of its lucrative operations. In April 1975, following the ERP's internal crisis that resulted in the deaths of Roque Dalton and Armando Arteaga, as well as in the attempted assassination of Ernesto Jovel, breakaway dissident elements of the ERP created a new organization called the Resistencia Nacional (RN), composed mostly of elements from the middle classes. The armed branch of the RN was the FARN.

Like the ERP, the FARN pursued a military revolutionary strategy of urban terrorism patterned after the model of the Uruguayan Tupamaros and the Argentine Montoneros. But unlike the ERP, it advocated the development of mass movements and solid political organizations as a complement to the military struggle.

One of the group's main characteristics was its penchant for kidnappings aimed not only toward gaining large ransoms but also toward making a political impact. For this reason, many of those kidnapped were foreign industrialists, such as Japanese businessman Fujio Matsumoto. As a result of this tactic, the FARN became the richest Salvadoran guerrilla group. Its coffers contained almost $75 million by 1980, according to some sources. In the late 1970s, in addition to undertaking several high-profile kidnappings, the FARN explained its demands through paid ads in Central American newspapers and even in the *New York Times*. It asserted the kidnappings would continue until democratic rights were restored in El Salvador.

In 1976, an alliance of peasants, students, and labor unions, the Frente de Acción Popular Unido—originally formed in 1974 and active for about six months—was reorganized as a front for the RN and the FARN. FAPU gained considerable influence in the urban unions and set up rallies and protests.

Urban terrorist actions by the FARN in the late 1970s included the assassinations of government sympathizers and members of paramilitary groups, especially the Organización Democrática Nacionalista (ORDEN, Nationalist Democratic Organization). By 1980, the FARN's strategy had moved more from the concept of resistance to an insurrectional approach.

In March of that year, the FARN joined the Directorio Revolucionario Unificado, the organization created to coordinate the actions of all Salvadoran guerrillas, and in October it became part of the Frente Farabundo Martí de Liberación Nacional, the Salvadoran guerrilla umbrella group created in 1982.

FUERZAS POPULARES DE LIBERACION— FARABUNDO MARTI (FPL)
Popular Forces of Liberation—Farabundo Martí

Active from 1970 to 1992; operated in the department of Chalatenango and in San Salvador; Maoist-Castrist; led by Salvador Cayetano Carpio, Sánchez Céren (aka "Leonel González"), and Mélida Anaya Montes (aka "Ana María"); supported by Cuba, the Soviet bloc, and Libya; represented by the front organization Bloque Popular Revolucionario (BPR, Popular Revolutionary Bloc).

In addition to being the oldest guerrilla group in El Salvador, the Fuerzas Populares de Liberación—Farabundo Martí was, until 1983, the largest one, with headquarters in Managua and political representatives operating mostly in Mexico and to a lesser extent in Costa Rica and Nicaragua.

On April 1, 1970, a minority dissident faction of the PCES, led by Salvador Cayetano Carpio, who had been secretary general until 1969, and Central Committee member "Ana María" Montes, broke with the party over its refusal to engage in rural guerrilla warfare and formally established the FPL.

Until the end of 1983, the FPL represented as much as one-third of El Salvador's total active guerrilla population. Since then, however, due to splits in the ranks and desertions, the group has dwindled to fewer than

2,000 fighters, becoming second in strength to the Ejército Revolucionario del Pueblo.

Despite its break from the Communist Party, the group sought to establish an economy along traditional Communist lines. Carpio's ideology evolved into a combination of Maoism and Castrism, and he advocated a guerra popular prolongada that would incorporate the peasantry as the key factor in a long-term, low-intensity conflict. Carpio was willing to use paralegal means and terrorism to achieve his goal but did not believe in the Salvadoran guerrillas' ability to successfully organize a general insurrection in the pattern of Nicaragua in 1979. On this matter, his views clearly clashed with those of the ERP and its leader, Joaquín Villalobos.

In the fall of 1972, the FPL launched its first terrorist actions, including attacks against the Argentine Embassy, to show its solidarity with the militants of the Argentine groups Montoneros and the Ejército Revolucionario del Pueblo killed trying to escape from the Trelew prison.

Until 1979, and despite the ostensibly rural base of its operations, the FPL's most spectacular and significant actions consisted in assassinations and kidnappings in San Salvador. It attacked national guard barracks and government installations and kidnapped several businessmen, government officials, and diplomats. Two of the group's most prominent victims were Foreign Minister Mauricio Borgonovo in 1977 and South African ambassador Archibald Gardner Dunn in 1979, both of whom were killed when the FPL's demands for ransom were not met.

After the FPL joined the FMLN, Carpio consistently refused to support the insurrectional tactics of other groups. Under his leadership, the FPL also disagreed with other guerrilla organizations over the FMLN campaign to disrupt the 1982 elections with popular uprisings. Carpio felt that his own FPL, rather than the umbrella FMLN, should be the vanguard organization of the Salvadoran revolution.

Carpio committed suicide in Managua in April 1983 in circumstances that have never really been clarified. Six days before his death, Montes had been assassinated by a group led by Rogelio Bazzaglia, an FPL leader close to Carpio. Leonel González succeeded Carpio as leader of the FPL, and Valentín Dimas Rodríguez was designated second secretary.

Following Carpio's death, the group, much weakened, redirected its guerra popular prolongada orientation. In line with other FMLN members, it began to advocate the idea of negotiating with the government in mid-1983 and/or staging an insurrection later that year. In late 1983, many FPL members expressed discontent, complaining of delayed payment of salaries, bad treatment, and lack of appreciation by higher-ups, and even middle-level and top-ranking leaders became disenchanted. After Carpio's suicide, the FPL lost influence in the FMLN and the ERP gained power.

The FPL's ability on the battlefield ranged from poor, as in the lackluster performance of its recruits during the 1981 Final Offensive, to significantly successful, as in the two attacks on the Brigade Headquarters in El Paraíso on January 1, 1984, and in 1987.

Its legal front organization, the Bloque Popular Revolucionario, created in 1975, included groups such as the Unión de Trabajadores del Campo (Union of Rural Workers) and the Asociación Nacional de Educadores Salvadoreños (National Association of Salvadoran Educators). The FPL considered an alliance between workers and peasants to be the necessary force for the struggle, with an emphasis on the peasants. Also, unlike the Frente de Acción Popular Unido, it discarded the possibility of alliance with the military and did not concentrate on working with the middle class.

PARTIDO REVOLUCIONARIO DE TRABAJADORES DE CENTROAMERICA/FUERZAS ARMADAS REVOLUCIONARIAS DE LIBERACION POPULAR (PRTC/FALP)
Revolutionary Party of the Workers of Central America/ Armed Revolutionary Forces of Popular Liberation

Formed in 1976; operated in San Salvador with some activity in the departments of Cuscatlán and La Unión; initially Trotskyist, but as of 1979 more orthodox Marxist-Leninist; led by Fabio Castillo Figueroa, Roberto Roca, Mario González, Ismael Dimas Aguilar, María Concepción Valladares, Luis Adalberto Díaz, and Humberto Mendoza; represented by the legal front organization Movimiento de Liberación Popular (MLP, Movement of Popular Liberation); gave up armed struggle in 1992.

The PRTC was established in San José, Costa Rica, on January 26, 1976, by Trotskyist elements from El Salvador, Honduras, Costa Rica and representatives from Guatemala and Nicaragua. The Salvadoran branch, which eventually came to number between 300 and 400, was made up of dissatisfied elements of the Fuerzas Armadas de Resistencia Nacional and the Partido Comunista de El Salvador and exiles from El Salvador living in Costa Rica.

The group's conception of the struggle was regional but rooted in the history of Central America. It did not surface in El Salvador until the last months of 1979, and until 1980 operations in Honduras, Guatemala, and El Salvador were linked together through funding and ideology. On October 29, 1980, the constituent national branches formally decided to become autonomous organizations operating independently of each other.

Initially, the founders of the PRTC turned to revolutionary violence because they were unhappy with the orientation of existing guerrilla groups in El Salvador. Until the Salvadoran branch joined the FMLN, its strategy was a combination of protracted war and flexible coalition.

As late as 1982, the PRTC was involved in urban terrorism patterned after the Tupamaros of Uruguay and the Montoneros of Argentina. It also acted in rural areas and attempted to infiltrate unions. After joining the FMLN, it participated in the peace negotiations brokered by the United Nations that resulted in the treaty of December 1992.

Bibliographical Commentary

Tommie Sue Montgomery's impeccably organized and researched *Revolution in El Salvador: Origins and Evolution* traces in thorough detail the development of guerrilla groups in the Central American nation until the early 1980s. For another well-researched, sympathetic portrayal of the guerrillas in that same time frame, consult Robert Armstrong and Janet Shenk's *El Salvador: The Face of Revolution. Bitter Grounds: Roots of Revolt in El Salvador*, by Liisa North, follows events into the middle of the decade, and subsequent developments are well documented in *The Dictionary of Contemporary Politics of Central America and the Caribbean*, edited by Phil Gunson, Greg Chamberlain, and Andres Thompson, as well as in innumerable press accounts from publications like the *New York Times. Latin American Insurgencies*, by Georges Fauriol, outlines efficient introductory sketches of each major group. *Times of the Americas* provides reports of the peace negotiations and the eventual peace signing. Because of its pronounced right-wing bias, *Latin American Revolutionaries: Groups, Goals, Methods*, by Michael Radu and Vladimir Tismaneanu, must be used with caution to cross-reference data.

Top: Enrique Gorriarán Merlo, ERP (undated), Argentina

Bottom: Former M-19 commander Rosemberg Pabón Pabón in his new life as a politician (early 1990s). Photo courtesy of *El País,* Colombia

Top: Militant priest Camilo Torres of the Colombian ELN (November 9, 1975). Photo courtesy of *El País,* Colombia

Bottom: Antonio Navarro Wolff, former commander of the M-19, interviewed in Cali during his campaign as a presidential candidate (April 13, 1994). Photo courtesy of *El País,* Colombia (Photographer: Orlando Blandón)

Carlos Pizarro León Gómez, leader of the M-19, gives up his weapon—wrapped in a flag of Colombia—during the ceremony to surrender arms (early 1990). Photo courtesy of *El País,* Colombia (Photographer: Osvaldo Paez)

An M-19 camp (undated). Photo courtesy of *El País,* Colombia (Photographer: Ernesto Guzmán)

Salvadoran guerrillas during peace negotiations in Oaxtepec, Mexico: Guadalupe Martínez (in right foreground), Roberto Cañas, Dagoberto Gutiérrez, Fermán Cienfuegos, and Salvador Samoyoa. Photo courtesy of *Diario Latino,* El Salvador (Photographer: Nelson López)

Shafik Jorge Handal, general secretary of the Communist Party and FMLN leader (undated). Photo courtesy of *Diario Latino,* El Salvador (Photographer: Nelson López)

93

Top: Joaquín Villalobos of the Salvadoran ERP (May 13, 1994). Photo courtesy of *Crónica* magazine, Guatemala (Photographer: Mario Robert Maras)

Bottom: Jorge Soto, aka "Pablo Monsanto," commander of the FAR (February 1994). Photo courtesy of *Crónica* magazine, Guatemala

Ricardo Rosales, aka "Carlos Gonzales," commander of the PGT-FAR (March 11, 1994). Photo courtesy of *Crónica* magazine, Guatemala

Rodrigo Asturias, aka "Gaspar Ilom," of Guatemala's ORPA (1993). Photo courtesy of *Crónica* magazine, Guatemala

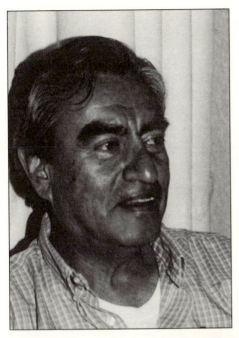

Top: Commander Rolando Morán of Guatemala's EGP (1993). Photo courtesy of *Crónica* magazine, Guatemala

Bottom: Sandinista commander Dora María Téllez speaks to workers at the Milca Bottling Plant in Managua (March 1981). Photo courtesy of *La Prensa,* Nicaragua

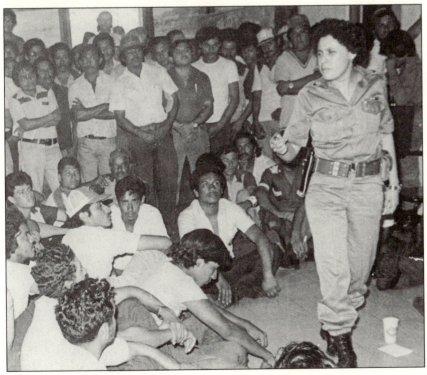

Sandinista fighters enter Managua in triumph (August 1979). Photo courtesy of *La Prensa*, Nicaragua

Sandinista Commander Tomás Borge (1982). Photo courtesy of *La Prensa*, Nicaragua

11

GRENADA

NEW JEWEL MOVEMENT (NJM)

Founded in 1973 from the merger of the Movement for Assemblies of the People and the Joint Endeavor for Welfare, Education, and Liberation; led by Maurice Bishop, Kendrick Radix, and Unison Whiteman; began organizing along Marxist-Leninist lines in 1974; seized power in 1979.

Along with the Cuban Movimiento 26 de Julio and the Nicaraguan Frente Sandinista de Liberación Nacional, the New Jewel Movement was the only other leftist group in the hemisphere to achieve power through revolution, though it was a left-wing political party that radicalized and not a guerrilla group.

A new political movement emerged in the 1970s in the non-Spanish-speaking Caribbean. The various groups, led by middle-class, foreign-educated intellectuals who had come of age in the time of Vietnam and the Cuban revolution, were generally socialist, anti-imperialist, and nationalist. One of these was the New Jewel Movement in Grenada. The NJM was born in 1973 from the merger of the year-old Movement for Assemblies of the People (MAP), led by Maurice Bishop and Kendrick Radix, and the Joint Endeavor for Welfare, Education and Liberation (JEWEL), led by Unison Whiteman and Selwyn Strachan, which had also been created in 1972.

Since the 1950s, the Grenadian political landscape had been dominated by former oil-field worker and trade union activist Eric Gairy. In 1967, Gairy and his Grenada United Labor Party returned to power for the third time, but his populist politics alienated the electorate. There was rampant corruption, and health and social services deteriorated. Prime Minister Gairy's men shot and killed Rupert Bishop, Maurice Bishop's father, during an opposition demonstration on June 21, 1974.

Soon after the island received independence, Gairy denounced the United Labor Party as "Communist," harassed the increasingly popular NJM, and briefly jailed Maurice Bishop.

The NJM secretly began to develop along Marxist-Leninist lines in 1974. Around this time, the movement produced the "Manifesto of the New Jewel Movement for Power to the People and for Achieving Real Independence for Grenada" (Sandford 1985: 15). The document called for an agricultural revolution, nationalization of hotels, and wage and price controls, among other things. By 1977 the NJM had made a complete transition from its initially nationalist origins to Marxist-Leninist principles. Bishop's deputy, Bernard Coard, became its leading ideologist and the head of the hard-line faction, the Organisation for Research, Education and Liberation (OREL).

After 1976, the group began infiltrating the established urban trade unions and formed an overseas network of support organizations to collect funds. It also tried to rally support among urban workers and increased its contacts with Cuba as it built a clandestine military wing, which would later become the People's Revolutionary Army (PRA).

On March 13, 1979, the PRA seized the army barracks, the police headquarters, and the police station. By the end of the day, Bishop and the NJM had taken control of the country. Gairy escaped arrest because he had left the day before for a United Nations meeting in New York.

Bibliographical Commentary

The New Jewel Movement: Grenada's Revolution, 1979–1983, by Gregory Sandford, offers a balanced chronological account of the birth and evolution of the New Jewel Movement and the historical context surrounding it. For a more succinct overview, consult *The Dictionary of Contemporary Politics of Central America and the Caribbean,* edited by Phil Gunson, Greg Chamberlain, and Andres Thompson.

12

GUATEMALA

EJERCITO GUERRILLERO DE LOS POBRES (EGP)
Guerrilla Army of the Poor

Active from 1972 to the present; operates in the northern highlands, El Quiché, Huehuetenango, Chimaltenango, and Alta Verapaz, with some activity in and around Guatemala City and the Ixcán region; embraced Marxism with ethnic overtones and subscribed to the concept of *guerra popular prolongada*; led by Rolando Morán (aka "Ricardo Ramírez") and Mario Payeras (aka "Benedicto"); connected to legal front organizations such as the Comité de Unidad Campesina (CUC, Committee of Peasant Unity) and church-based radical groups, among them the Frente Popular 31 de Enero (FP-31, Popular Front January 31st), the Unidad Revolucionaria Nacional Guatemalteca (URNG, Guatemalan National Revolutionary Unit), and Central Unificada Campesina (Unified Peasant Union); severely decimated by the government counterinsurgency campaign of 1982.

The Ejército Guerrillero de los Pobres was first active in the northwestern highlands in January 1972. Its leaders, Rolando Morán and Mario Payeras, entered Guatemala from Chiapas, Mexico. From their initial position, the group moved on two fronts east and west in the northern Quiché.

Formed by a nucleus of survivors of an offshoot of the Fuerzas Armadas Rebeldes who were critical of *foquismo* and subscribed to the concept of *guerra popular prolongada*, the EGP soon became the most significant of the new breed of Guatemalan revolutionary groups that emerged in the 1970s and became arguably the strongest guerrilla group in Guatemala until the early 1980s.

It placed a strong emphasis on Guatemalan politics and society and in bonding with the peasantry. Learning from the mistakes of their predecessors, these revolutionaries sought to maintain a low profile and carefully built a base in the highlands before engaging in any open activity.

EGP leaders refused to get involved in ideological disputes in order to better concentrate on the immediate demands and needs of peasant communities. Partially because of security reasons and partially because of its objective of winning the hearts and minds of peasants, the EGP leadership did not grant interviews. Its leaders waited until 1981 to publish anything about its objectives.

The basic strategy of the EGP was to incorporate the masses through popular education and the political formation of peasant communities. This approach was a departure from the strategy of earlier groups, which did not focus on Indian areas but hoped to ignite revolution by working from pockets of activities called "focos." The new approach was partly based on the lessons learned from revolutionary Ernesto "Che" Guevara's experience in Bolivia: Small guerrilla groups in the jungle, without the support of a peasant base, will always be on the run. Thus, the group slowly began developing contacts in peasant villages by doing small favors for the peasants. The approach enabled the group to tap into the discontent produced by the greediness of local landlords. Moreover, as more commanders and members came from indigenous groups, peasant support was more easily gained.

The first EGP military action took place in the Ixcán when hated landlord Luis Arenas Barrera, the "Tiger of Ixcán," was killed in public on payday in 1975. By the end of 1976, the EGP controlled several areas of the northern highlands. In Guatemala City, the group claimed responsibility for the November 6 bombing of a hotel in retribution for the killing of two EGP members by the hotel owner's security guard.

The military reacted with a brutal counterinsurgency campaign in the Quiché region. Local organizations were attacked and, by 1977, more than 100 village leaders in the Ixil area of El Quiché had been killed. The fact that all peaceful avenues to change appeared closed served to heighten support for the guerrillas. On December 31 of that year, EGP guerrillas kidnapped a former minister. He was released on January 30, 1978, after the following demands were met: the publication of an EGP manifesto, payment of a large ransom, and safe conduct granted to an EGP member who had sought refuge in the Costa Rican Embassy.

Much of the EGP support from the Alta Verapaz and areas of the Quiché dated from the May 29, 1978, army massacre at Panzós in response to Indian protests over land seizures. Official estimates stated that forty-three peasants had been killed and seventeen wounded in the army's action. In Guatemala City, a June 8 march protesting the slaughter was followed by an EGP bombing that killed fourteen military police on June 14.

Also contributing to the growing political consciousness among the poor was the massacre that occurred in Guatemala City in 1980. A group of twenty-two peasants had come to the city to protest the military occupation of their villages, to demand the release of seven village leaders that the military had kidnapped, and to call for the formation of a commission to investigate the actions of the military. While there, they heard reports that the seven San Miguel Uspantán leaders had been found dead in Chajul. Seeking sympathetic support, the peasants, along with student and worker supporters, decided on a peaceful occupation of the Spanish Embassy. On January 31, 1980, the police stormed the building, killing thirty-nine people.

The consequences of the Spanish Embassy incident also fueled the revolutionary struggle. Some of the peasants killed in the embassy came from the town of Nebaj. Consequently, the army occupied that community, detaining some 3,000–4,000 peasants in the marketplace. When women from neighboring villages came to inquire about their husbands, the military fired on them, killing at least eleven. This incident was considered to be another turning point for the EGP as many villagers began to join its forces.

In the late 1970s and early 1980s, the EGP became a formidable political and military force with significant military apparatus and a large peasant following. However, it barely survived virtual eradication in the 1980s. From July to November 1980, the EGP carried out fifteen ambushes and seventeen attacks on barracks, outposts, and other fixed positions. Another significant event of that year was the September 5 announcement by Elías Barahona, press secretary at the Guatemalan Ministry of the Interior, that he was a member of the EGP who had infiltrated the government four years earlier. He asserted that Guatemala's president, General Romeo Lucas García, and the minister of the interior were directly responsible for commanding the death squads.

In 1981, the EGP showed its support for the Comité de Unidad Campesina, the first major Guatemalan peasant organization, when its members staged a raid to free kidnapped CUC leader Emeterio Toj Medrano from the army barracks. This daring action also helped increase the EGP's popular support. During the early 1980s, the EGP controlled much of the countryside, entering highland villages at will to hold political discussions and gather recruits. In June 1981, the group claimed to have advanced its war to nineteen of Guatemala's twenty-two departments, concentrating on the oil region of Verapaz.

During this period, the government responded with an intense counterinsurgency war initiated by Lucas García and consolidated under General José Efraín Ríos Montt. The goal was to remove the peasant base from the guerrillas, or "drain the sea" (Jonas 1991: 149). The campaign entailed brutal repression against all popular organizations and development groups. In addition, four EGP members were the first guerrillas to be executed judicially under military rule in 1982.

The counteroffensive hit the EGP hard. Not only were three of its guerrilla fronts obliterated but also internal problems developed within the organization. By 1985, Payeras's differences with Morán had become insurmountable, and Payeras was expelled from the EGP.

On February 8, 1982, the EGP joined the Organización Revolucionaria del Pueblo en Armas, the Fuerzas Armadas Rebeldes (FAR, Rebel Armed Forces), and a faction of the Partido Guatemalteco del Trabajo (PGT, Guatemalan Labor Party) to form the Unidad Revolucionaria Nacional Guatemalteca (URNG, Guatemalan National Revolutionary Unit) umbrella group. Its purpose was to pursue a "popular revolutionary war" in order for the people "to free themselves from oppression, exploitation, discrimination and dependence on foreign countries" (Degenhardt 1983: 366). The four participating groups decided to maintain their distinct structures. Although the EGP was a political and military unit, it also claimed that it was "a popular army which will support whatever government is substituted for the tyrannical one" (Handy 1984: 250).

In 1984, following the most intense period of the government's counterinsurgency campaign, EGP forces renewed their actions, announcing that in that year they had carried out 181 operations and killed 686 government troops. In 1985, they claimed to have 4,000 armed and 12,000 unarmed members. The URNG was seeking political participation within a democratic framework, but EGP commander Morán added that democracy "must not be understood only as a mechanism for elections" (Barry 1992: 76).

The 1985 Guatemalan Constitution barred all guerrilla groups from participation in elections, and it was not until 1990 that peace talks were initiated between the URNG and the country's different political and military sectors. By 1992, the talks seemed to be little more than a political tactic for the government as it waited out the hoped-for demise of the guerrilla forces.

The URNG's negotiations for a dismantling of the repressive state apparatus, including the country's notorious civil patrols, and respect for human rights have been continually rejected by the government. In addition, the government of Jorge Serrano Elías rejected any substantive United Nations participation in the URNG-government dialogue, claiming that the UN would violate Guatemalan sovereignty. Under President Ramiro de León Carpio, the peace process resumed with significant activity in March 1994, but a peace treaty has not yet been signed.

FUERZAS ARMADAS REBELDES (FAR)
Rebel Armed Forces

Active from 1960 to the present, with periods of dormancy; its main areas of operation initially were the eastern regions of Izabal and Zacapa, later Guatemala City and the Indian highlands; currently concentrated most heavily in El Petén and northern Alta Verapaz; initially nationalistic and anti-imperialist with evolution into Marxism-Leninism; led by Luis Alberto Turcios Lima (who was killed in a car crash in 1966), Marco Antonio Yon Sosa (who died in 1970), César Montes, and Jorge Soto (aka "Pablo Monsanto"); maximum strength estimated at 500 fighting cadres; destroyed by government in the late 1960s and early 1970s; regrouped and reemerged in the late 1970s; obtained arms mainly from raids on Guatemalan Army installations, bank robberies, and kidnapping ransoms; periodically represented by Partido Guatemalteco del Trabajo.

Fuerzas Armadas Rebeldes, the oldest guerrilla organization in Guatemala, has military origins. After President Jacobo Arbenz Guzmán was deposed in 1954, Colonel Carlos Castillo Arms took over. He was shot in 1957 by one of his palace guards, and in the elections of 1958 General Miguel Ydígoras Fuentes came to power.

By 1960, the Central Intelligence Agency was training Cuban exiles on a coffee plantation in Retalhuleu for the Bay of Pigs invasion. On November 13 of that year, young military officers with nationalist aspirations, and not hostile to Fidel Castro, led an uprising because of the government's decision to allow Guatemalan territory to be used for this military training.

Although the revolt was suppressed in barely four days, it allowed progressive elements in the military to establish alliances with students, workers, and peasant groups. It also afforded recognition to this faction's main leaders—Colonel Rafael Sessan Pereira, Captain Marco Antonio Yon Sosa, Lieutenant Luis Alberto Turcios Lima, and Colonel Alejandro de León—the men who would become chief rebel commanders. Ironically, Yon Sosa and Turcios Lima were graduates of U.S. counterinsurgency training programs at Fort Gulick in Panama. After their failure, the rebels fled to exile (Pereira to Mexico, Yon Sosa to Honduras, and Turcios Lima to El Salvador) and were helped by peasants in their escape.

On February 6, 1962, Yon Sosa, Turcios Lima, and Luis Trejo Esquivel went back into action in the mountains of Izabal in the Sierra de las Minas. They called themselves Movimiento Revolucionario Alejandro de León 13 de Noviembre (Revolutionary Movement Alejandro de León November 13th). The first part of the name paid tribute to their comrade, Colonel Alejandro de León, who was part of the original group of rebels but was captured and killed in July 1961. The date commemorated the initial revolt. Their first actions were an attack on army outposts in Bananera and Morales and the robbery of a United Fruit Company office.

Meanwhile, riots, strikes, and student demonstrations continued in Guatemala City in response to allegedly rigged congressional elections. Several political parties called for Ydígoras's resignation. Lasting until April, the guerrilla revolt and the urban agitation were quelled after the military dictator ordered a massive army crackdown, forcing the rebels to retreat to the countryside to reorganize.

On March 30, 1963, Colonel Enrique Peralta Azurdia overthrew Ydígoras, who tentatively had been preparing for constitutional elections. The coup, which diminished the possibility of creating democratic rule, made guerrilla struggle an increasingly viable option. Under Peralta Azurdia, the Communists and other political parties were banned.

During 1963 and 1964, the guerrillas went from a nationalist, anti-imperialist orientation to an acceptance of Marxism as a method of analysis and action. The group began calling itself only Movimiento Revolucionario 13 de Noviembre (MR-13, Revolutionary Movement November 13th) and used Alejandro de León as a front organization led by Yon Sosa. Another front, led by Turcios, took the name Edgar Ibarra.

Both fronts worked together, combining military and social action among the peasantry. They initially pursued a common Guevara-style foco strategy, relying on the spontaneous politicization of the population surrounding a guerrilla center of operations. The revolutionary vanguard at this center would serve as a catalyst to galvanize the people of the countryside to follow the guerrillas' example. Although the movement included students and members of the Partido Guatemalteco del Trabajo, it had a very strong peasant component. Operations included assaults on police stations, bank robberies, and kidnappings of leading capitalists and diplomats.

But as early as October 1964, Yon Sosa and Turcios Lima were diverging ideologically. Their operations in the eastern regions of Izabal and Zacapa adopted increasingly separate military strategies and political objectives. Yon Sosa distanced himself from the PGT. Influenced by Mexican Trotskyist Amado Granados, he called for the immediate establishment of "liberated zones" in which the guerrillas would govern. Turcios Lima's closer ties to the PGT were consistent with his belief in a Cuban-style revolution that would draw support from the middle class. He argued that this objective could be achieved through a gradual process of winning over the hearts and minds of the Guatemalans. Havana supported Turcios Lima and sharply rebuked Yon Sosa for his Trotskyist inclinations. Turcios Lima formally disassociated from the MR-13 in March 1965 and allied with the PGT's guerrilla front to form the Fuerzas Armadas Rebeldes.

Insurgent activity continued unabated despite the growing disunity. On February 9, 1965, the chief of the U.S. military mission, Colonel Harold Houser, was shot at in his car while driving home. MR-13 claimed responsibility. In May, the deputy minister of defense, Colonel Ernesto Molina Arreaga, was shot dead outside his home. Several wealthy Guatemalans were kidnapped in November and December.

The split with Yon Sosa did not resolve problems of infighting under Turcios Lima's command. When César Montes, a member of the PGT's Central Committee, was chosen second-in-command, he sought to cultivate closer ties with the leadership of the PGT. This development produced tension between those who favored maintaining Turcios Lima's army contacts and focusing on military objectives and those who emphasized the electoral process as a means of advancing the struggle.

The rift was exacerbated by the perception among some FAR members that the candidates for the 1966 elections included a viable option for Guatemala's progressive forces. This alternative was the Partido Revolucionario's (Revolutionary Party's) presidential candidate, Julio César Méndez Montenegro. A former law professor of the FAR's César Montes, Méndez won the official endorsement of the PGT. The FAR's position on the Méndez candidacy was less than enthusiastic. At the January 1966 Tricontinental Conference in Havana, Turcios Lima denounced the "hollowness" of the "electoral game" and asserted that it was inappropriate for true revolutionaries to support a candidate in the election.

While Turcios Lima was away in Havana, however, the FAR issued a statement supporting the Méndez candidacy. When Turcios Lima returned, he did not reverse this official stance.

Surprisingly, Méndez Montenegro defeated the two colonels who challenged him for the presidency and took power on July 1, 1965. The FAR's response to the Méndez victory was to embark on a partial demobilization, although no formal truce had been declared.

Because the new civilian leadership was of popular derivation, the revolutionary armed struggle lost some of its appeal, but the FAR hoped to retain support by arguing that the army still had most of the effective power. The guerrilla thinking was not that far off, as subsequent events showed. Indeed, in order to pacify the military, Méndez allowed it a free hand in the extermination of the guerrillas and allowed U.S. troops to begin assisting in anti-insurgency campaigns. The dramatic increase of U.S. support for the military's mission, particularly the influence of U.S. Green Beret Special Forces, was a significant factor in decimating the guerrillas. In addition to extensive training, the United States provided direct military assistance in the form of aerial bombings and napalm raids carried out from U.S. bases in Panama. Meanwhile, in Guatemala City, right-wing paramilitary brigades such as Mano Blanca (White Hand) and Consejo Anticomunista de Guatemala (Anti-Communist Council of Guatemala) escalated in strength and scope.

Already suffering from the loss of Turcios Lima, who was killed in a car accident in October 1966, FAR guerrillas and their suspected sympathizers were no match for the energetic army counterinsurgency campaign, even though Yon Sosa rejoined the FAR as its head in late 1967, bringing with him a number of other ex-Trotskyists from the MR-13.

Also, the FAR initially had neglected the country's indigenous population. Some rebel leaders were disdainful of the Indian majority, and others expected that no direct appeals would be necessary for this alienated group to take up arms against the ruling powers. Not until the end of the 1960s did FAR strategists realize that a more concerted effort would be required to gain favor with Guatemala's twenty-two indigenous groups. By this time, the FAR's political and military strength had been greatly diminished. Once strong in the countryside, the FAR was forced to abandon comprehensive rural warfare for sporadic urban attacks and kidnappings.

In 1968 the group announced its formal separation from the PGT from a camp in the Sierra de las Minas. On January 16, 1968, FAR guerrillas shot Colonel John Webber, head of the U.S. military mission, as well as the naval attaché. Shortly afterward, U.S. ambassador John Gordon Mein was killed in a botched kidnapping attempt.

Following Turcio's death, the army initiated a relentless counterinsurgency campaign. Within a few months the Edgar Ibarra front was destroyed, and subsequently the Alejandro de León front was annihilated. Yon Sosa was captured and killed in 1970.

The FAR never officially conceded total defeat. Although in the late 1970s it managed to regroup and reemerge, the FAR was unable to remain the dominating guerrilla organization in Guatemala, since new guerrilla movements formed that were more effective in organizing the country's indigenous majority. Still, it retained a reputation as one of the country's most consistently militaristic and hard-line groups.

After joining the URNG, the umbrella group, in 1982, the FAR's current commander, Pablo Monsanto, was among the least willing to offer concessions in the peace negotiations. Yet, in mid-1991, he acknowledged the implausibility of achieving the group's revolutionary goals via armed struggle. Consequently, he approved the URNG's emphasis on "gaining political participation and achieving objectives within the democratic framework" (Barry 1992: 70). Still, the group remained at the negotiating table within the URNG. Under the government of President Ramiro de León Carpio, these negotiations advanced intermittently through 1994 and 1995, but peace has not been established.

ORGANIZACION REVOLUCIONARIA DEL PUEBLO EN ARMAS (ORPA)
Revolutionary Organization of the People in Arms

Initiated activities in 1971; operates in Guatemala City, the departments of Sololá (around Lake Atitlán), Quetzaltenango, San Marcos, and Suchitepequez; embraces a combination of Marxism, Leninism, Maoism, and the ideas of Franz Fanon and José Carlos Mariátegui, with a heavy indigenist component; led by Rodrigo Asturias Amado (aka "Gaspar Ilom") and Julia Solórzano Foppa; still active at present.

After periods of dormancy and urban terrorism in the late 1960s, various offshoots of the Fuerzas Armadas Rebeldes reemerged in the 1970s, primarily in the Indian-populated highlands. Among these groups was the Organización Revolucionaria del Pueblo en Armas, which was created in Mexico in 1972 by Rodrigo Asturias Amado, son of Nobel laureate Miguel Angel Asturias, as well as the remaining members of the FAR's Regional de Occidente, a dissident group that split from the parent group in 1971 over revolutionary strategy, believing that the FAR's position regarding the Indian question was racist and that Indians were key to the revolutionary struggle.

In June of that year, the ORPA began its first efforts to establish a rural base of support through an indoctrination program aimed at Indians. By September the dissidents had formally broken with the almost defunct FAR. Along with the EGP, the ORPA became the strongest of the Guatemalan guerrilla groups, with the FAR and the Communists fielding numerically inferior forces.

From the outset, the ORPA, along with the Colombian M-19, was perhaps the least ideological, most pragmatic, and most un-Marxist of Latin American guerrilla groups. The ORPA, like the EGP, developed strong bases of peasant support and recruitment in the Indian highlands of western Guatemala, focusing mainly on indigenous populations in San Marcos, Totonicapán, Quetzaltenango, and Sololá, especially around Lake Atitlán. Both groups altered their pure Marxist theories to fit the existing circumstances, "insisting that under Guatemalan conditions they were pursuing not just a class-based socialist revolution but also a national revolution of 'Indians' against their Spanish oppressors." They met and recruited Indians through the medium of Indian languages such as Kekchi and Mamand Cakchiquel. As Wickham-Crowley points out, guerrilla combat units came to be composed largely of Indians—in some cases as much as 99 percent. There is also evidence of female participation in this guerrilla group.

Initially the membership was 90 percent indigenous and rural, but in the early 1970s the ORPA organized within the urban labor movement and emphasized the need for alliances with intellectuals and professionals. Its maximum strength is estimated at 2,000.

The ORPA was oriented more toward a militaristic approach to revolution than a combined political, mobilizational, and militarist one. For this reason it has not paid much attention to the establishment of significant front organizations, although at the end of 1972 it did establish an urban network.

The ORPA refrained from direct action for about eight years during the early to mid-1970s but went public in 1979, when on September 18, it occupied a coffee farm in Quetzaltenango. In June 1981, ORPA guerrillas operating in groups of up to 200 people occupied towns in San Marcos, Retalhuleu, and Huehuetenango.

As an individual movement, the ORPA grew through 1982, when General Efraín Ríos Montt, a born-again Christian, pursued a violent counterinsurgency campaign to put an end to guerrilla activity. Ríos Montt himself was overthrown by General Humberto Mejía Victores in 1983. Still, the anti-guerrilla operations continued through 1984. During this period, the army killed tens of thousands of peasants in the highlands in the name of counterinsurgency. The 1984 election of a Constituent Assembly ostensibly paved the way for civilian rule, but the ultimate power remained with the army. The ORPA managed to stay alive despite setbacks and joined the URNG, which is presently negotiating for peace with the government of President Ramiro de León Carpio, in 1982.

PARTIDO GUATEMALTECO DEL TRABAJO/FUERZAS ARMADAS REVOLUCIONARIAS (PGT-FAR)
Guatemalan Labor Party/Revolutionary Armed Forces

Active from 1968 to the present; armed branch of the Partido Guatemalteco del Trabajo; Marxist-Leninist; led by Ricardo Rosales (aka "Carlos Gonzalez").

The Partido Guatemalteco del Trabajo, Guatemala's Communist party, was founded in 1949 and took its present name in 1951. It was banned after Jacobo Arbenz's overthrow in 1954 and has remained illegal ever since, although it has retained an influential role in the Guatemalan labor movement.

In 1961, while General Miguel Ydígoras Fuentes was in power, the PGT came out in support of armed struggle. It eventually joined forces with the Movimiento Revolucionario 13 de Noviembre, and the two coalesced to form the Fuerzas Armadas Rebeldes in 1962. The PGT was assigned the political leadership of the group and in that role gradually withdrew its support of armed struggle.

In January 1968, a formal break occurred between the FAR and the PGT, with the former accusing the Communists of supplying the ideas while they supplied the combatants. The PGT's response was to form its own FAR. The acronym was the same as Turcios Lima's FAR, but the "R" stood for "Revolucionarias" (Revolutionary) instead of "Rebeldes" (Rebel). The new FAR was to serve as the armed branch of the PGT.

In 1966, and again in 1972, the bulk of the PGT leadership was captured and murdered by the armed forces. By the mid-1970s the PGT-FAR had formally abandoned guerrilla warfare, a development that led to serious splits in the ranks. In 1981, the Núcleo de Dirección Nacional (NDN, Nucleus of National Leadership) broke from the PGT over the issue of armed struggle, and in 1982 it helped found the Unidad Revolucionaria Nacional Guatemalteca. Throughout the early 1980s, the PGT was paralyzed by this infighting, but by the mid-1980s the NDN and the Central Committee of the PGT had come to operate as one and aligned with the URNG.

As part of the URNG, the PGT-FAR is participating in peace negotiations with the government of President Ramiro de León Carpio.

UNIDAD REVOLUCIONARIA NACIONAL GUATEMALTECA (URNG)
Guatemalan National Revolutionary Unit

Guerrilla umbrella group founded in 1982 and still active today, with a maximum estimated strength of 3,000; led by Rolando Morán (aka "Ricardo Ramírez"), Pablo Monsanto, Rodrigo Asturias Amado, and Carlos González; engaged in peace negotiations with the government of Guatemala.

This guerrilla front was founded in January 1982 by the Ejército Guerrillero de los Pobres, the Fuerzas Armadas Rebeldes, the Organización Revolucionaria del Pueblo en Armas, and the Partido Guatemalteco del Trabajo/Fuerzas Armadas Revolucionarias around a five-point program.

In a statement, *Guatemala, the People Unite!* the group outlined the following objectives: the elimination of repression against the people; the guarantee to all citizens of human rights; representation in government of all "patriotic, popular and democratic sectors"; the resolution of the fundamental needs of the great majority through the elimination of the economic and political domination of the wealthy, both national and foreign, who rule Guatemala; the guarantee of equality between Indian and *Ladinos* (whites) and the end of discrimination; and a policy of non-alignment and international cooperation, which poor countries need in order to develop in the modern world.

The four guerrilla forces united in the URNG decided to maintain distinct philosophies and operate in different regions. A fusion of their military forces did not take place until early 1985, when the Comandancia General (General Command) was set up.

By 1982, as a result of the brutal counterinsurgency campaign pursued first by General Romeo Lucas García and later by his successor General Efraín Ríos Montt, the guerrilla movement in Guatemala took very serious losses. The URNG remained on the defensive until the mid-1980s, but it gradually recovered, and despite the government's continual counterinsurgency campaigns the guerrillas were operating near the capital in 1989.

The URNG announced that it would not seek to disturb government reform efforts provided that democracy was the real intention of the elected government. Increasingly through the 1980s, the URNG focused on the political rather than the military aspects of the struggle.

In May and October 1986, the guerrillas proposed preliminary negotiations with President Vinicio Cerezo and called for an army purge. Cerezo expressed his willingness to engage in talks but said that the guerrillas would have to lay down their arms before any negotiations could take place. The guerrillas refused to accept this condition.

The URNG repeated its call for talks in February 1987, but it was again rebuffed, first by the army and then by the government. Following the signing in August 1987 of the Central American Peace Accords (known as the Arias Plan after Costa Rican president and Nobel Peace Prize recipient Oscar Arias), which prescribed negotiations for all three countries involved in civil wars, the URNG extended its offer once again.

This time Cerezo agreed to preliminary talks between the URNG and the Comisión de Reconciliación Nacional (Commission of National Reconciliation) set up for the purpose. In October 1987 talks were held in Madrid between the government and the guerrillas, with army officers present as observers, but these were accompanied by an intensification of military activities on both sides.

Inconclusive meetings were held in Costa Rica in late 1988 and early 1989. Dialogue resumed in 1990 in various locations, including Mexico. The government of Jorge Serrano Elías did not achieve any significant milestones, but the government of Ramiro de León Carpio, which took over in 1993 after Serrano Elías was overthrown by the army, achieved significant progress in March 1994.

Bibliographical Commentary

As the longest-running insurgency in the hemisphere, Guatemala has received periodic scholarly attention. In *Inside Guatemala*, Tom Barry presents an excellent introductory sketch of all major groups, as does

Henry Degenhardt as the editor of *Revolutionary and Dissident Movements: An International Guide*. Richard Gott's *Guerrilla Movements in Latin America* and *Rural Guerrillas in Latin America* follow in great detail the history of Fuerzas Armadas Rebeldes from origin to annihilation. Susanne Jonas's *The Battle for Guatemala: Rebels, Death Squads and U.S. Power*, although clearly sympathetic to the guerrillas, offers a balanced treatment of the development of the Guatemalan insurgency from its origin until 1991 in a traditional scholarly format that includes analysis as well as chronological account. From a decidedly leftist perspective and using a somewhat melodramatic style, Vania Bambirra, Alvaro Lopez, Moisés Moleiro, Silvestre Condoruma, Carlos Nuñez, Ruy Mauro Marini, and Antonio Zapata reflect on the first ten years of guerrilla activity in *Diez años de insurreción en América Latina*, as does João Batista Berardo in *Guerrilhas e guerrilheiros no drama da América Latina*. Timothy Wickham-Crowley discusses the insurgencies from a sociological viewpoint in the intensively researched and erudite *Guerrillas and Revolution in Latin America: A Comparative Study of Insurgents and Regimes Since 1956*. *Guerrillas in Latin America: The Technique of the Counter-State*, by Luis Mercier Vega, also devotes space to discussion of the Guatemalan guerrilla.

13

HONDURAS

FRENTE MORAZANISTA DE LIBERACION NACIONAL HONDURENA (FMLNH)
Morazanist Front of Honduran National Liberation

Active from 1967 to the present; operates mainly in the major cities of Honduras; Maoist ideology; consists of a few hundred cadres; led by "Octavio Pérez"; supported by Nicaragua, Cuba, and Libya.

The precise starting date of the Frente Morazanista de Liberación Nacional Hondureña, formed by a small splinter group of the Partido Comunista de Honduras (PCH, Communist Party of Honduras), is difficult to establish, but it was clearly sometime after the 1967 breakup of the party's Maoist and Muscovite branches. The Frente Morazanista was the armed wing of the Maoist faction, which established the Partido Comunista Hondureño-Marxista Leninista. The Frente's goal was to take power by armed force. Its spokesman, "Octavio Pérez," claimed that the FMLNH was created on September 16, 1969.

Sporadically active in the 1960s and 1970s, the group was reestablished in September 1979 in the wake of the overthrow of Anastasio Somoza in Nicaragua. Just prior to the 1980 elections, which put Liberal Party candidate Roberto Suazo Córdova into office but in reality left the military in control, the Frente Morazanista announced its intention to engage in armed struggle once the "electoral farce" was over (Radu and Tismaneanu 1990: 283).

In July 1989 and then again in April 1990, the Frente claimed responsibility for the assassination of several activists of the Frente Unido Universitario Democrático (FUUD, Democratic United University Front) in San Pedro Sula for alleged connections between this institution and military intelligence. It also attacked U.S. military personnel stationed in the central department of Comayagua.

It joined the Directorio Nacional Unido—Movimientos Revolucionarios Hondureños (DNU-MRH, United National Directorate—Honduran Revolutionary Movements), an umbrella organization, but it undertook no joint action with other members of that alliance.

In May 1990, the Morazanistas announced they were abandoning armed struggle, but they were active as late as October 5, 1991, when they claimed responsibility for the assassination in San Pedro Sula of Raúl Suazo of the FUUD, a right-wing activist reportedly associated with military intelligence agencies.

FUERZAS POPULARES REVOLUCIONARIAS LORENZO ZELAYA (FPR-LZ)
Popular Revolutionary Forces Lorenzo Zelaya

Active from 1981 to the present; operates in Tegucigalpa and San Pedro Sula; Sandinista-Marxist; led by Efraín Duarte Salgado; supported by the Nicaraguan Sandinistas, the Guatemalan Organización Revolucionaria del Pueblo en Armas (ORPA), and radical Mexican groups.

The Fuerzas Populares Revolucionarias was founded on November 30, 1980, and an armed wing was established called the Lorenzo Zelaya Command, named after a peasant leader active in the Frente de Acción Popular (Popular United Front) who was killed in 1965 in the department of Yoro.

The group, with a maximum estimated strength of fewer than 100 cadres, is made up of students from the Universidad Nacional who advocated prolonged, popular, revolutionary war. But because of its small size and lack of popular support, the organization has been limited to attacks on high-visibility targets such as embassies and foreign companies.

Its first significant actions were the shooting of two U.S. military advisers and the bombings of the Chilean and U.S. Embassies on October 31, 1981, as well as numerous similar attacks in the early 1980s. On August 4, 1982, the organization claimed responsibility for a bomb attack against the Tegucigalpa offices of TACA Airlines of El Salvador, Air Florida, and IBM. In addition, FPR leader Efraín Duarte Salgado was captured by authorities that year. After negotiations with the government, he was allowed to emigrate to Guatemala.

In 1983, the FPR joined the umbrella organization of the Honduran insurgency movements, the Directorio Nacional Unido—Movimientos Revolucionarios Hondureños, but it undertook no joint actions.

An attempt to infiltrate guerrillas from Nicaragua in 1984 led to exposure of part of the FPR network. The Honduran government claimed that the FPR amounted to nothing more than an extension of the Nicaraguan Frente Sandinista de Liberación Nacional (FSLN, Sandinista National Liberation Front), charging that the group was intent on publicizing the presence of anti-Sandinista Nicaraguans on Honduran soil. According to some versions, Salvadoran guerrillas also undertook terrorist acts in Honduras in order to raise funds for their struggle. In February 1987, the Froylán Turcios Front of the FPR claimed responsibility for two bombings, one of them directed at the home of Nicaraguan contra leaders. Two weeks after these attacks, Honduran security forces executed a couple whom they claimed were Lorenzo Zelaya leaders.

Under the government of President Rafael Leonardo Callejas, the FPL published a communiqué in the newspaper *Tiempo* on April 28, 1991, calling on the government to promulgate an unconditional amnesty and release all political prisoners. The group said it would renounce armed revolution in favor of civic struggle but also demanded the dismantling of the national intelligence forces.

MOVIMIENTO POPULAR DE LIBERACION "CINCHONEROS" (MPL-Cinchoneros)
Popular Movement of Liberation "Cinchoneros"

Active from 1980 to the present; Marxist-Leninist, populist rural; most spectacular operations were the hijacking of an airliner in 1982 and the occupation of the San Pedro Sula Chamber of Commerce, taking eighty-three hostages, in the same year; linked to Salvadoran guerrilla groups; maximum strength estimated at fewer than 100 cadres.

The Movimiento Popular de Liberación Cinchoneros was an offshoot of the Partido Comunista de Honduras and was named after a peasant leader's profession (a *cinchonero* is a saddle-stropper maker). The folk leader Serapio Romero was a cinchonero who organized an uprising in 1865 using a strategy similar to the one the MPL was to follow.

Of student origin, the Cinchoneros began to coalesce in 1978 when some members of the PCH decided that the reformist approach the party had been taking was pointless. The movement was founded on March

26, 1980, and its approach to armed struggle was similar to that of the Salvadoran Fuerzas Populares de Liberación. Some versions go as far as stating that the Cinchoneros were actually established by the Salvadorans as a nucleus for violence and support in arms trafficking. Indeed, during 1981, seven Salvadoran guerrillas from the Ejército Revolucionario del Pueblo undertook a three-month training and restructuring of the Cinchoneros.

The Cinchoneros advocated guerra popular prolongada as well as hit-and-run operations and sabotage. Their first known operation took place on February 4, 1981, and involved the explosion of a homemade leaflet bomb in front of the Metropolitan Cathedral in Tegucigalpa. But the group also lost several key leaders that year. Its main leader, Fidel Martínez (aka "Comandante Antonio"), was considered officially disappeared after March 1981.

In 1982, the Cinchoneros not only successfully hijacked an airliner to free political prisoners but also undertook the operation that put them on the map: For eight days in September 1982, they held eighty-three members of the San Pedro Sula Chamber of Commerce hostage, including the Honduran ministers of finance and the economy. Their demands included the release of political prisoners and the expulsion of foreign military advisers. The government of President Roberto Suazo Córdova refused to negotiate, except to offer the guerrillas safe conduct out of Honduras. The guerrillas eventually flew to Cuba, with an intermediate stop in Panama. Many allegations exist that Honduran security forces had heavily penetrated the revolutionary cell and used it to artificially create an atmosphere of crisis on occasion.

Around this time there were numerous reports of human rights violations in Honduras and the Suazo Córdova government was accused of sponsoring institutionalized repression. The rebels saw his government as a puppet of U.S. imperialism and Honduras as the springboard for an invasion of Nicaragua by anti-Sandinista forces.

Like other Honduran guerrilla groups, the Cinchoneros joined the Directorio Nacional Unido—Movimientos Revolucionarios Hondureños but undertook no joint operations with other Honduran guerrilla groups.

In January 1989, the Cinchoneros claimed responsibility for the murder of former armed forces chief General Gustavo Alvarez Martínez. In August 1990, many exiled Cinchoneros returned to Honduras under an amnesty program launched by President Leonardo Callejas. The group has not been active lately.

PARTIDO REVOLUCIONARIO DE TRABAJADORES CENTROAMERICANOS—HONDURAS (PRTCH)
Revolutionary Party of Central American Workers—Honduras

Active from 1977 to the present; initially Trotskyist, but by 1980 it had lost this ideological emphasis; operates regionally with branches in various Central American countries; led by José María Reyes Matta, Wilfredo Gallardo Museli, and Father James Hanley Carney (aka "Padre Guadalupe"); supported by Cuba and Nicaragua.

The Partido Revolucionario de Trabajadores Centroamericanos—Honduras was founded on February 20, 1977, as a regional organization committed to carrying on the revolutionary process in El Salvador, Guatemala, Costa Rica, and Honduras. In Honduras it took no action for six years other than participation in politics, although by 1980 it was already banned.

The party was largely a creation of radical elements of the Universidad Nacional Autónoma de Honduras (National Autonomous University of Honduras). It launched its armed struggle in May 1983, arguing that a single vanguard movement had to be formed at the regional level.

In its biggest action, the Olancho operation, carried out under the command of José María Reyes Matta in July 1983, the group enabled almost 100 Nicaraguan guerrillas to infiltrate Honduras. This two-month plot ended in defeat with ninety-four out of ninety-seven Honduran guerrillas killed, captured, or defecting. Reyes Matta and James Carney, the group's chaplain—a U.S.-born priest who had been expelled from Honduras in 1979 for subversion—were said to have died, although their bodies were never produced. The following year, the PRTCH attempted a similar operation, with the same results.

In 1983, the PRTCH announced the formation of the Directorio Nacional Unido—Movimientos Revolucionarios Hondureños, which supposedly also comprised the Morazanistas, the Cinchoneros, and the Fuerzas Populares Revolucionarias Lorenzo Zelaya. No joint actions were subsequently undertaken.

Bibliographical Commentary

Material on Honduran guerrilla groups is very scarce and sketchy. In *Latin American Revolutionaries: Groups, Goals, Methods*, Michael Radu and Vladimir Tismaneanu come up with a fairly detailed portrayal of the movements, but their right-wing ideological bias undermines the credibility of their material. *The Dictionary of Contemporary Politics of Latin America and the Caribbean*, edited by Phil Gunson, Greg Chamberlain, and Andres Thompson, Georges Fauriol's *Latin American Insurgencies*, and *Latin American and Caribbean Contemporary Record*, Volume 2, edited by Jack W. Hopkins, all include specific but scanty data. Although containing virtually no references to insurgency, Alison Acker's *Honduras: The Making of a Banana Republic*, as well as *Honduras: A Country Study*, edited by James D. Rudolph, are useful for a general socioeconomic and historical view of the country.

14

MEXICO

EJERCITO ZAPATISTA DE LIBERACION NACIONAL (EZLN)
Zapatista Army of National Liberation

Initiated activity in 1994 with the occupation of four towns and several villages in the southern state of Chiapas; ideology combines a Guevarist foquista strategy with demands for the disenfranchised; strength estimated at 2,000; "Subcomandante" Marcos is its visible head.

On January 1, 1994, the day of the inauguration of the North American Free Trade Agreement, the Ejército Zapatista de Liberación Nacional seized four towns and several villages in Chiapas. One of these towns was San Cristóbal de las Casas, which, with a population of 90,000, is the state's second largest city.

The rebels began to withdraw into the mountains the following day. Within one week they had given up all the communities they had taken over, but the armed uprising still left 145 soldiers and Indians dead.

The Zapatistas have a strong Indian component, and its rank and file is made up mostly of Mayans of the Tzeltzal and Tzotzil groups. According to one observer, however, the organization was not originally conceived that way. The Zapatistas had been trying to create a rural foco, but gradually adapted themselves to their environment. Their tactics, with the emphasis on recruiting popular support, seems the most effective ever by a Mexican insurgency group.

Militarily, however, the Zapatistas did poorly, chalking up only one near-success—the assault on a garrison outside San Cristóbal—in their initial armed action.

Twelve days after the New Year's Day takeover of San Cristóbal de las Casas, President Carlos Salinas announced a unilateral ceasefire. A tentative agreement was reached during talks in February between

EZLN representatives and the government's peace commissioner, Manuel Camacho Solís, a member of the ruling Partido Revolucionario Institucional and former mayor of Mexico City. Both sides agreed to a thirty-two-point program affecting political and economic issues in Chiapas as well as human rights concerns for Mexico's indigenous populations.

But the Zapatistas called a halt to those talks because of a basic lack of trust in the government promises. After suspending the dialogue the guerrillas retreated to their stronghold, the Lacandón jungle region near the border with Guatemala.

Throughout 1994, the EZLN was sporadically active, while the government remained on the negotiation track. In February, 1995, however, the government changed its tactics. Where his predecessor Carlos Salinas had stressed negotiations, President Ernesto Zedillo now embarked on an offensive aimed at discrediting the rebel commanders by launching a public relations war to "unmask" them in order to reveal their middle-class background. The arrest of six Zapatista leaders was ordered, including that of "Subcomandante" Marcos, who was identified as Rafael Sebastián Guillén, a former college professor and son of a furniture salesman.

Zedillo also decided to rely once again on the use of force and ordered the army into Chiapas to take back the territory occupied for the previous thirteen months by the Zapatistas. As a result, some public buildings were reopened and patrols were set up throughout much of the region. The army units advanced deep into Chiapas, scattering thousands of campesinos to the mountains.

On May 14, 1995, both sides began the first formal talks in over a year. After fifteen hours of deliberations, the government and the Zapatistas jointly announced plans to ease tensions and move toward peace negotiations. The EZLN proposal called, among other things, for the regrouping of army troops strung along major roads in the areas where the Zapatistas are active, to be replaced with armed rebels who will be responsible for patrolling the area.

Although negotiations continue, no definitive peace accord has been reached.

LIGA COMUNISTA 23 DE SEPTIEMBRE (L-23)
Communist League September 23rd

Active from 1973 to 1976; ultra-Marxist-Leninist; operated in Mexico City, Guadalajara, Monterrey, and Sinaloa, and to a lesser extent in Chihuahua, Oaxaca,

Sonora, and Tamaulipas; made up mostly of students and university professors and teachers; maximum strength estimated at around 800 armed cadres; led by Ignacio Salas Obregón, Manuel Gámez, Gustavo Hiroles Morán, David Jiménez Sarmiento, José Angel García, and Rosalbina Garabito; supported itself through bank robberies and kidnappings.

The Liga Comunista 23 de Septiembre was formed by members of other organizations that had disbanded, including armed groups like the Movimiento de Acción Revolucionaria (Movement of Revolutionary Action), whose militants trained in North Korea, and the Frente Estudiantil Revolucionario (Revolutionary Student Front) of Guadalajara. These groups had become active in 1969 and the beginning of the 1970s.

Two of the groups, Juventud Comunista (Communist Youth) and the Cristianos Socialistas de Monterrey (Socialist Christians of Monterrey), were particularly alienated from the Partido Comunista Mexicano (Mexican Communist Party), which had virtually come apart in 1968 when most of its leadership had landed in prison and was considered weak and ineffectual.

The Liga was made up mostly of students and some university professors and teachers, most of lower middle-class extraction. Its main leader, Ignacio Salas Obregón, came from the Cristianos Socialistas. Ironically, he was not a Communist but a Hegelian Christian. In addition to the 800 armed cadres, the ranks of the Liga included more than 2,000 sympathizers and supporters.

The group's main goal was total subversion of the established order. Following an uncompromisingly extremist line, it never sought to establish a dialogue with the government but instead hoped to install Communism with no intermediate steps. The organization supported armed struggle as a catalyst and as preparation for the real armed struggle once the proletarian army was formed.

The Liga was founded by twelve militants who, in March 1973, became members of the Dirección Nacional (National Leadership), the directing body of the organization. These militants were never associated with the USSR. Nor did they have links with Cuba, partly because the ruling Partido Revolucionario Institucional had always maintained cordial relations with revolutionary Havana and partly because of ideological divergences with Castro. The Liga was strictly a national phenomenon, with no contacts overseas, and was very xenophobic and mistrustful of foreign organizations.

It also failed to make connections with other Mexican groups. The cadres were extremist and out of touch with Mexican reality, and they aimed to persuade other groups of the validity of the Liga's position rather than to seek alliances. The Liga referred to more moderate groups as "reformists" and called for them to abandon union activism and join the armed struggle, even though the Liga itself pursued political activities.

The movement's goals and plan of action were laid out in the first three issues of *Madera,* the Liga's newspaper, and in the *Manifiesto al estudiantado proletario* (Manifesto to the Proletarian Student Body).

The Liga's most spectacular coup was the kidnapping of Eugenio Garza Sada in Monterrey in September 1973. Another important kidnapping was that of the British consul in Guadalajara.

However, the lack of proper tactical and strategic preparation often led to failure. On January 16, 1974, in an insurrection in Culiacán, some 100 guerrillas arrived in the city and took over the armory. Their goal was to rob the banks and leave. At the same time, another group was trying to agitate some 3,000 peasants. What started as a *jornada de agitación y combate* (day of agitation and combat) got out of control, and an army battalion was sent in from Mexico City. The ensuing fight lasted some four or five hours, leaving some twenty peasants and militants dead.

In addition to inadequate planning, the Liga's own extremism and intransigence were key factors in its downfall. Efforts to create rural armies in Oaxaca, Chihuahua, and Sonora were doomed because the militants' vision was too radical for the locals. Besides, the guerrillas who went to the countryside soon found themselves cut off from their urban comrades and adopted a rural lifestyle in the mountains.

The group fared no better in urban areas. At first its activism had been welcome in factories, but the Liga's radicalism eventually alienated workers. Also, without a coherent strategy, Liga activists became very predictable and easily infiltrated by police.

Initially, the government had been willing to negotiate, but Liga militants equated negotiation with treason. After the kidnapping of Garza Sada, the government hardened its position and discarded the option of dialogue. Salas Obregón was captured and executed by the armed forces.

The death knell for the movement sounded with the death of David Jiménez Sarmiento in 1976 during the attempted kidnapping of the sister of then president José López Portillo.

Even before this incident, however, the movement had been disintegrating. Many other groups had abandoned armed struggle as a viable option, and several factions within the Liga were pressuring the group to abandon violent action as a means of change. Jiménez Sarmiento led the faction that continued to support armed struggle.

From the reformist side of the Liga emerged the Corriente Socialista (Socialist Current), which became the Partido Patriótico Revolucionario (Revolutionary Patriotic Party), now a faction of the Partido Revolucionario Democrático (Democratic Revolutionary Party). Other elements of the Liga returned to the fold of the Communist Party or joined the Trotskyist Party.

PARTIDO REVOLUCIONARIO DE OBREROS Y CAMPESINOS/PARTIDO DE LOS POBRES (PROCUP/PdlP)
Revolutionary Party of Workers and Peasants/Party of the Poor

PdlP founded circa 1969–1974; PROCUP/PdlP union occurred in 1975; Marxist-Leninist; operated in the states of Oaxaca and Guerrero before 1975, and after that in Oaxaca, Guerrero, and Mexico City; PdlP led by Lucio Cabañas (killed in 1975); PROCUP led by David Cabañas, who also led the organization after the group merger; former Oaxaca University director Felipe Martínez Soriano is alleged to be in a leadership position, but his lawyers deny such a connection.

Founded in Western Mexico by Lucio Cabañas in 1969, the Partido de los Pobres was briefly active in the Guerrero mountains in the early 1970s until 1975, when Cabañas was killed in a shootout with police. It never had more than eighty fighters.

In 1975, his brother, David Cabañas, founded the Partido Revolucionario de Obreros y Campesinos and merged the group with the PdlP. Activity continued into the late 1970s and early 1980s, with numerous bombings reported in 1977. In 1984 the group kidnapped Mexican Communist Party leader Arnaldo Martínez Verdugo and held him for seventeen days.

Following the kidnapping, PROCUP/PdlP was inactive until April 2, 1990, when the militants staged an attack on the offices of *La Jornada*, a Mexican daily critical of the group. Two guards were killed in the attack, though the group later stated in an editorial in that paper that the "lamentable occurrences on April 2 were not part of a strategy or tactics, but were an act of chance" ("Mexican Guerrilla Group Lashes Out at Leftist Newspaper," 1990). Subsequently, three members of the group, including David Cabañas and Felipe Martínez Soriano, were arrested in

Mexico City. Police had charged Martínez Soriano with leading the attack, but he denied any connection between himself and PROCUP. The guerrillas who were arrested complained of being tortured by police.

In reprisal, the group executed a June 1990 bombing in southeastern Mexico. No deaths or injuries resulted. Further, the group abducted a German consular official in Oaxaca in late October of that year, successfully calling for the release of Martínez Soriano.

August 1991 saw a new series of bomb attacks in Mexico City. Police blamed the first one, carried out against a Citibank office in Mexico City on August 11, on PROCUP, though no official claim of responsibility was called in. On August 15, 1991, members claimed responsibility for three bombings in Mexico City of an IBM office, a McDonald's restaurant, and a Mexican chain restaurant. There were no casualties. Those claiming responsibility explained the bombings as part of a campaign to stop police torture of PROCUP/PdlP members in custody. But jailed party leaders urged that the campaign of violence be abandoned, as Mexico's National Human Rights Council had given assurances that the instances of torture would cease.

On June 28, 1992, Martínez Soriano was arrested and again charged with involvement with PROCUP/PdlP. Martínez, head of the Frente Nacional Democrático del Pueblo (National People's Democratic Front), a legally recognized opposition party, reportedly has had his political enemies assassinated by PROCUP hit squads.

In July 1993, local ranchers showed government investigators and reporters pamphlets supposedly issued by PROCUP. The ranchers claimed that PROCUP members were training in their area and requested increased police presence. Critics charged that the claims were false and theorized that they had been manufactured to discourage peasant protests for land reform.

Bibliographical Commentary

Almost nothing has been written on a scholarly level about Mexican guerrilla groups. Most of the information available can be found in contemporary press reports.

15

NICARAGUA

FRENTE SANDINISTA DE
LIBERACION NACIONAL (FSLN)
Sandinista National Liberation Front

Active in the armed struggle from 1961 to 1979, when it toppled the government of Anastasio Somoza and seized power; embraced a combination of Marxism Theology of Liberation and Sandinismo, emphasizing a vanguard role for the Frente Sandinista de Liberación Nacional; most spectacular operation was the attack in 1974 of a Christmas party at the home of a Somoza associate; led by Tomás Borge, Carlos Fonseca, Silvio Mayorga, Henry Ruiz, Jaime Wheelock, Daniel Ortega, and Humberto Ortega; supported by the USSR, Cuba, Costa Rica, and Mexico; represented by legal front organizations such as the Frente Estudiantil Revolucionario (FER, Student Revolutionary Front).

In nineteenth-century Nicaragua, the upper classes, consisting of coffee growers, cattle ranchers, and merchants, amassed large fortunes. The ruling elite's power was divided, however, between the Liberal and Conservative Parties. This division weakened Nicaragua to the extent that neither party could resist meddling from the United States in the latter half of the century. U.S. Marines subsequently occupied Nicaragua in the 1920s and the 1930s, and private Americans exploited the country's resources with little respect for Nicaraguan interests.

The only viable opposition to the U.S. presence came from General Augusto César Sandino, who led a small guerrilla force from 1926 to 1934. Sandino was a militant nationalist who pledged to fight until the Marines left Nicaragua. When the U.S. forces left in 1934, Sandino agreed to lay down his arms but was lured to the presidential palace on February 21, 1934, and murdered by U.S.-backed Anastasio Somoza García and his National Guard. Somoza soon established a firm dictatorship with severe repression. Although popular guerrilla movements had little success from 1934 to 1956, while the country was under Somoza's rule, Sandino's name would not be forgotten.

In 1956, a poet named Rigoberto López Pérez assassinated Anastasio Somoza García, marking the beginning of a new period of guerrilla activity in Nicaragua. López's action introduced to Nicaraguans a new form of opposition to the government. Somoza García's son, Anastasio Somoza Debayle, came to power and imposed a brutal repression of opposition political leaders.

But López already had planted the revolutionary seed. Nicaraguan students, notably Carlos Fonseca Amador, began to revive Sandino's writings and ideology. Inspired by revolutionary Ernesto "Che" Guevara and the successful Cuban revolution of 1959, high school and university students began to mobilize in opposition to Somoza.

In July 1961, Fonseca met with two fellow students, Tomás Borge and Silvio Mayorga, in Tegucigalpa to discuss the creation of a national liberation movement to overthrow the Somoza regime. The result was the establishment of the Frente Sandinista de Liberación Nacional. Sandino's struggle and his nationalistic beliefs became the ideological centerpiece of the group. Originally called the Frente de Liberación Nacional, it changed its name to FSLN in 1963 to honor Sandino.

Originally, the FSLN concentrated its activities in the mountains, rallying peasant support for the Sandinista ideology, which called for the removal of Somoza and the creation of a new society that would apply Marxist ideals to the Nicaraguan reality. FSLN leaders believed that only guerrilla life in the mountains could mold ordinary peasants into legitimate revolutionaries. By endorsing this approach, however, the FSLN failed to win the support of the masses and suffered devastating initial defeats at Río Coco and Río Bocay.

Because its first armed actions, launched in 1963 from Honduras, were unsuccessful, from 1963 to 1967 the FSLN began to concentrate on generating urban support for its cause. With few members and scarce resources, the Sandinistas had trouble rousing enthusiasm among the urban poor but managed to acquire a substantial student following through the Frente Estudiantil Revolucionario, a Sandinista-backed university student organization founded in 1962. With FSLN support, the FER expanded to eventually include Nicaraguan high school students. Nevertheless, by concentrating their efforts in the cities, the FSLN was then unable to maintain a strong following in the countryside and still failed to become a viable political force.

After evaluating the failures of the mid-1960s, Fonseca and the FSLN leadership devised a new strategy, guerra popular prolongada, which focused on long-term goals to be accomplished with the support of the rural proletariat and a war of attrition.

In 1966, the FSLN decided to resume the military aspect of its social revolution. The Sandinistas began to form and strengthen guerrilla units around the mountain of Pancasán, near Matagalpa. They also integrated peasant recruits with the regular guerrilla formations to create an organized fighting force in the center of the country.

However, the National Guard detected the guerrilla columns in August 1967 and launched a full-scale attack, killing thirteen Sandinistas, including Silvio Mayorga. Although a critical military setback, Pancasán became a political victory for the Sandinistas. The organization received considerable publicity because of this episode and used it to portray the military conflict as part of a larger social uprising.

In addition, the movement once again tried to gain support in the urban barrios. On July 15, 1969, however, the National Guard attacked an FSLN safe house in Managua, killing five Sandinista militants. The attack exposed the Sandinista weakness in the cities, and the FSLN leadership ordered the organization to go underground in 1970. During this period, the Frente relied on intermediate organizations such as the FER to maintain support among the students and in factories.

The 1970s would see the FSLN grow from an organization of a few dozen members into a large-scale, successful revolutionary movement, partially because of an event that the Sandinistas did nothing to bring about. The devastating Managua earthquake of 1972 sparked another rise in the popularity of the Frente. The quake destroyed Nicaragua's capital city, killing more than 10,000 people and leaving over 250,000 homeless. Somoza, rather than devoting himself to repairing the city, used the earthquake for personal gain, defalcating many of the relief funds coming into the country from overseas donors. As his popularity declined, the FSLN quietly gained strength in the countryside.

On December 27, 1974, the Frente broke almost five years of silence with a successful attack on a Christmas party at the Managua home of José María "Chema" Castillo, a Somoza confidant. The Sandinistas took several government officials hostage and exchanged them for a dozen Sandinista prisoners, a $1 million ransom, and a broadcast of the Sandinista manifesto. As a result of the attack, Somoza lost the respect of much of the citizenry and the common people saw that popular opposition could be effective against the dictatorship.

The Somoza regime responded to the 1974 attack with a brutal reign of terror. With the aid of U.S. military advisers, Somoza imposed martial law, suspended constitutional guarantees, and began a campaign to eliminate the rebels that eventually caused the deaths of approximately 3,000 peasants in the countryside.

The FSLN was again forced into hiding, although this time with a broader base of public support. Because communication between the cities and the mountains was nearly impossible, the FSLN divided into three factions. The first faction was the Tendencia Proletaria (TP, Proletarian Tendency), led by Jaime Wheelock and Luis Carrión, which split in 1975 and favored the vanguard role of the proletariat and the need for a Marxist-Leninist party. The second tendency was the rural Guerra Popular Prolongada (GPP, Prolonged Popular War), which believed in the central role of both rural and urban forces, which would coalesce gradually. It was headed by Henry Ruiz and Tomás Borge. The third group was the Tendencia Insurreccional (Insurrectional Tendency), or the Terceristas. This faction, under the leadership of Daniel and Humberto Ortega and Víctor Tirado López, favored an immediate insurrection. Each group had three representatives each on the Directorio Nacional (National Directorate), a body designed to voice the concerns of all the revolutionary factions.

In November 1976, Fonseca Amador was killed. By 1977, the Directorio Nacional clearly favored the Tercerista strategy and launched a new series of operations. With the help of some distinguished exiled Nicaraguan intellectuals, mainly living in Costa Rica, called the Grupo de los Doce (Group of Twelve), the Terceristas began to mobilize mass support for their cause. Although Somoza continued his unremitting repression, support for the Frente continued to grow.

Another critical turning point for the Sandinistas, and again an event they did nothing to bring about, occurred on January 10, 1978. Pedro Joaquín Chamorro, editor of *La Prensa* and a leading opposition figure, was assassinated by a Somoza cabal. The Chamorro murder sparked mass demonstrations, a general strike, and broader support for the FSLN cause. In response to the demonstrations, the National Guard beat and then shot students as well as members of the general public. A particularly dramatic protest occurred in the Indian community of Monimbo, where the Indians suffered hundreds of casualties.

By February 1978, more isolated insurrections identified with the Sandinistas had broken out. In June, the three factions signed agreements favoring immediate insurrection and establishing a national Sandinista coordinating committee. Next, the FSLN created the Movimiento del Pueblo Unido (MPU, Movement of the United People) and joined with a variety of political and civic organizations to develop a concrete plan for mass opposition to Somoza. The MPU also pressured Somoza into allowing the exiled Grupo de los Doce to return to Nicaragua. In a remarkable display of support for the Sandinistas, more than 150,000 people showed up to welcome the exiles home.

In August 1978, the Sandinistas attacked the National Palace and seized the building, along with approximately 1,000 hostages. The Somoza government met the Terceristas' demands, which included the release of key FSLN leaders. The Sandinistas became national heroes, and the revolution reached the masses.

The National Guard temporarily contained the rebellion, but the FSLN had already won a crucial political victory and could no longer be denied. The Frente carried the momentum gained from the September mass insurrection into the political arena, and the people's support for the movement became a force too strong for Somoza to suppress. The FSLN created an alternative political structure called the Frente Patriótico Nacional (FPN, National Patriotic Front), which adopted the three fundamental elements of the Sandinista program—disbandment of the National Guard, nationalization of Somocista business and property, and establishment of a democratic popular government. The FSLN also created Radio Sandino to link the rural guerrillas with the urban militias. As the communications network became better established, the Sandinistas prepared for the final offensive.

The offensive took place in three phases in 1979. From May 29 to June 8, the Sandinistas attacked Somoza on all fronts, using popular insurrections simultaneously with general strikes. From June 9 to June 25, the Frente fought the battle of Managua, bringing critical international attention to its cause. In the third phase, from June 26 to July 12, the Sandinistas took Carazo and consolidated the northern cities. The offensive was completed with unprecedented success.

Finally, Somoza realized the hopelessness of his situation. He abandoned the capital on July 17 with what was left of the public funds, and the FSLN took power after two decades of struggle.

Bibliographical Commentary

Dennis Gilbert's *Sandinistas: The Party and the Revolution* is a comprehensive treatment of the Sandinista ideology and the progress of Sandinistas from subversives to country rulers. Gary Ruchwarger, in *People in Power*, concentrates mostly on postrevolutionary events but in a strongly pro-Sandinista tone devotes significant attention to the unfolding of the revolutionary struggle. The Sandinistas also received considerable coverage in the popular press. The *New York Times* can be consulted for both Sandinista movements and news analysis.

16

PARAGUAY

FRENTE UNIDO DE LIBERACION NACIONAL (FULNA)
United Front of National Liberation

Active briefly in the early 1960s.

In the beginning of 1960, revolutionary focos supported by Havana sprang up in the regions of San Pedro, General Aquino, and Rosario under the name of Frente Unido de Liberación Nacional. The coalition, which included members of the Communist Party, infiltrated a small group of seventeen rebels into Paraguay from Brazil and attacked the village of Capitán Bado. The local police repulsed them, and a few days later they were wiped out by the army. A second attempt was made by a larger force of approximately 200 guerrillas who attempted to establish a base in the jungle along the Upper Paraná River but were found by the army and destroyed. A third invasion, on December 20, 1960, was also a failure. After this defeat, FULNA abandoned armed struggle.

Bibliographical Commentary

There is virtually no scholarly treatment of Paraguayan insurgency. Most of the above information was culled from Paul Lewis's *Paraguay Under Stroessner.*

17

PERU

EJERCITO DE LIBERACION NACIONAL (ELN)
Army of National Liberation

Active from 1962 to 1965; Castrist; used Trotskyist revolutionary Hugo Blanco's brand of guerrilla warfare; operated in the department of Ayacucho, particularly the province of La Mar; led by Héctor Béjar Rivera, Juan Zapata Bodero, and Ricardo León; supported by Cuba.

The Peruvian Ejército de Liberación Nacional emerged from a split within the Partido Comunista Peruano (PCP, Peruvian Communist Party). Disgusted with the bureaucratic style of the Communists, ELN founders, which included former members of the Communist Party and radical students, came to believe that only revolutionary struggle would create a new type of Communist Party. It advocated guerrilla warfare in rural areas but also favored underground activities in cities.

In May 1963, some thirty-five guerrillas entered Peru from Bolivia but were dispersed after a clash and subsequent manhunt, in which poet Javier Heraud was killed. The bulk of the guerrillas survived and left the country. Upon their return to Peru they contacted non-Trotskyist elements of the Frente Izquierdista Revolucionario (FIR, Revolutionary Leftist Front) and created the Movimiento 15 de Mayo (M-15, May 15th Movement), in memory of the day Heraud was killed.

Later they provided cadres for the ELN, a movement led by journalist Héctor Béjar, a former member of the Communist Party who had been expelled on charges that he was a Trotskyist. His group operated in Ayacucho beginning in September 1965. For the two previous years, Béjar had worked among peasants in Huanta, forming the nucleus of the ELN. He had also tried to integrate its forces with those of the Movimiento de Izquierda Revolucionaria (MIR, Movement of the Revolutionary Left), but he could not overcome his ideological differences with Luis de la Puente Uceda.

In its first action, the ELN took over some private property, but the army reacted promptly. On December 17, 1965, two of Béjar's lieutenants, Juan Zapata Bodero and Ricardo León, were killed in an armed encounter. After this defeat, the ELN lost its influence and became a marginal segment of the far Left. Béjar himself was jailed in 1966.

On October 3, 1968, a coup brought General Juan Velazco Alvarado to power. Béjar, who was released from prison, actively collaborated with Velazco Alvarado in 1969.

FRENTE IZQUIERDISTA REVOLUCIONARIO (FIR)
Revolutionary Leftist Front

Initiated activity in 1961; Trotskyist with elements of democratic radicalism; operated in the Valle de la Convención, department of Cusco; led by Hugo Blanco; represented by the legal Partido Obrero Revolucionario (POR, Revolutionary Workers' Party); leader Hugo Blanco became a fugitive and was captured by the authorities in 1963; politically active at present, although with a marginal influence.

Primarily a peasant organizer, Hugo Blanco supported the ideas of Argentine Trotskyist Hugo Bressano (aka "Nahuel Moreno"), who had been Blanco's professor at the University of La Plata in Argentina and who advocated the strong buildup of a party to mobilize the masses.

After studying abroad, Blanco returned to Peru in 1956 and joined the Trotskyist Partido Obrero Revolucionario. Although anti-Chinese and pro-Cuban, Blanco opposed Ernesto "Che" Guevara's foco theory as a vehicle to revolution. He advocated the need for worker-peasant alliances and assumed political agitation would help peasants claim the land and lead to armed struggle.

In 1958, Blanco traveled for the first time to the Valle de la Convención in Cusco to organize urban workers and expand the POR apparatus. But he switched from workers to peasants and began organizing them from a base as a subtenant farmer. Within three years he had formed 148 unions, although only six had existed in the region before his arrival. A year later, he started off with strikes as a means of vindicating demands.

As delegate of the Departmental Peasants' Federation in Cusco, Blanco became secretary in charge of agrarian reform. He launched into de facto expropriations of landowners from the department and decreed that tenants and subtenants were the owners of the land they cultivated. A peasant militia was organized and guerrilla units, with an estimated strength of some 100 cadres, were formed. Blanco's slogan was "Land or Death."

In view of these developments, the POR held a congress in 1960 to draw up an insurrectional program in the form of guerrilla warfare. The party decided to create a revolutionary front, the Frente Revolucionario (FR, Revolutionary Front), to unite the Peruvian Left. In Cusco the FR was created in June 1961, and the Frente Izquierdista Revolucionario was born in December from the union of POR, the Juventud Comunista (Communist Youth), and other groups.

To raise funds for the armed struggle, the FIR committed two bank robberies, one in 1961 and another in 1962, when funds promised by the Trotskyist movement in Argentina failed to materialize.

The revolt was scheduled for June 10, 1962. Due to differences with the Lima directorate and the Trotskyist movement in Argentina, Blanco was left alone. He continued to organize, but the armed forces repressed his efforts. In November 1962, Blanco and some of his peasant followers attacked a small police station and Blanco killed a member of the civil guard at the post.

Blanco became a fugitive and was captured on May 29, 1963. Although initially sentenced to twenty-five years in jail, he was released after serving seven years under a political amnesty declared by President Juan Velazco Alvarado. Blanco then proceeded to become a candidate for the Constituent Assembly in 1978 and won a seat.

In the late 1970s, the FIR joined an alliance of ultraleftist groups, but in March 1979, significant differences surfaced between Blanco and Genaro Ledesma, an important leftist leader. By mid-1979, the Partido Socialista de los Trabajadores (Workers' Socialist Party) had been expelled from the front for promoting Blanco's presidential ambitions.

MOVIMIENTO DE IZQUIERDA REVOLUCIONARIA (MIR)
Movement of the Revolutionary Left

Initiated activity in 1962; Marxist, Mariateguista, and Castro-Guevarist, with certain Maoist elements (like participation of the peasantry); led by Luis de la Puente Uceda, Guillermo Lobatón, and Ricardo Gadea; supported by Cuba; destroyed by the armed forces in 1965.

From 1959 to 1966, next to the two major parties, there existed several left-wing forces in Peru. A dissident group, influenced by the Cuban revolution and headed by Luis de la Puente Uceda, split from the Alianza Popular Revolucionaria Americana (APRA, Popular Revolutionary American Alliance) and evolved into the Movimiento de Izquierda Revolucionaria.

The leaders of the MIR were young intellectuals of middle-class origin. Ideologically, the group was closer to Beijing than to Moscow. In October 1959, de la Puente Uceda founded APRA Rebelde (Rebel APRA), a group that tried to implement agrarian reform through legal channels and was briefly associated with Hugo Blanco's Frente Izquierdista Revolucionario. After considerable harassment, including an unrelated jail sentence, de la Puente Uceda abandoned the Aprista affiliation in 1962 and created the MIR, which began the armed struggle in July 1965.

De la Puente Uceda expounded the theories of Hugo Blanco and embraced Blanco's guerrilla strategy. However, nothing came of a meeting between the two leaders in 1964. Even though de la Puente Uceda advocated mainly rural, protracted guerrilla warfare, he wanted to mobilize not only the peasantry but also progressive elements of the bourgeoisie.

In its 1965 offensive, the MIR did not employ the flexible foco theory. Instead, it settled into a series of immobile security zones. In its revolutionary proclamation to the Peruvian people, issued from the mountains in June of that year, the MIR talked about three insurrectional focos and called upon the parties of the Left to support it.

One of its fronts, Guerrilla Pachacutec, was headed by de la Puente Uceda himself and operated mainly in the south. Another front was the Guerrilla Tupac Amaru, which operated in the center of the country under the leadership of Guillermo Lobatón. A third front, Guerrilla Manco Capac, was active in the north. Its commanders were Gonzalo Fernández Gazco and Elio Portocarrero Ríos.

Attempts to coordinate the actions of these groups with those of the Ejército de Liberación Nacional ultimately failed. However, the fronts carried out a number of successful strikes. Starting July 7, Tupac Amaru attacked a group of civil guards and robbed them of their weapons. Two days later, after stealing several trucks, the insurgents stormed the armory in Santa Rosa, taking twenty-two boxes of dynamite and 2,100 explosives, with which they later destroyed a bridge over the Manayniyoce and burnt some farms. Simultaneously, another Tupac Amaru commando attacked a civil guard outpost in Andamarca. On July 18, power plants were sabotaged and more bridges destroyed. The guerrillas also began recruiting peasants, sharing their booty with them. In Lima, starting in July, bombs were detonated in theaters, hotels, bars, and cafes, while in Arequipa, public utilities warehouses were raided for dynamite.

In the mountains, the guerrillas repeatedly beat the army in encounters such as the battle of Kubainta on August 9. Pachacutec, encouraged by Tupac Amaru, also began a series of violent attacks. Meanwhile, the MIR and the Partido Obrero Revolucionario multiplied their calls to armed struggle at the University of San Marcos in Lima.

On August 20, the government declared the death penalty for any subversive act. The armed forces began a methodic siege of Mesa Pelada, a guerrilla stronghold. On October 23, 1965, they killed de la Puente Uceda and destroyed the Pachacutec unit.

After its initial successes, Tupac Amaru suffered some setbacks. Its attack against the army barracks in Pucuta on September 22–23 failed. The leader of the front, Máximo Velando Gómez, was captured on December 7 and executed, and Lobatón died in a clash on January 7, 1966.

Ricardo Gadea emerged as the new leading figure within the MIR after the deaths of de la Puente Uceda and Lobatón. Gadea, a hard-line Castrist, was arrested after the uprising in 1965 and set free in 1970. But the MIR never recovered from the death of de la Puente Uceda. It reemerged in the early 1970s and was officially reformed in 1977, but armed struggle was no longer part of its agenda. During the late 1970s, it maintained a strong Castrist orientation, and in October 1980, it joined a bloc of Peruvian left political parties, the Izquierda Unida (United Left).

MOVIMIENTO REVOLUCIONARIO TUPAC AMARU (MRTA)
Tupac Amaru Revolutionary Movement

Active from 1984 to 1993; combined indigenism (Tupac Amaru, Manco Inca, and so on) with radical populism, Mariateguismo, and Castrism and Guevarism as modified by the Sandinista experience; operated in the northeast (the Huallaga valley and the departments of Cajamarca and Lambayeque) and urban areas, including Cusco, Lima, and Arequipa; maximum strength estimated at 500 cadres; led by Víctor Polay Campos, Peter Cárdenas, Andrés Mendoza, José del Aguila Valles, Marco Antonio Turkowsky, Ernesto Montes Aliaga, Pedro Mires Samaniego, Néstor Canchari Villena, Félix Calderón Olazábal, and Luis Varese Scotto.

The organizational structure of the Movimiento Revolucionario Tupac Amaru was established in Lima in 1975 by elements of the Movimiento de Izquierda Revolucionaria, and the group subsequently began recruiting members. The MRTA originally focused on urban guerrilla warfare, although it claimed to represent the peasantry.

By 1981, the MRTA's infrastructure had developed into zonal and later regional commands. Its first action, only two years later, was the robbery of the Banco de Crédito in Lima on May 31, 1982. On November 6, 1983, the group adopted its present name, and by June 1984, the various factions and splinters were unified.

In 1983, the MRTA took over the Lima offices of the United Press International news wire service, and over the next few years the group seized various local and national radio and press organizations, which it used to spread its revolutionary message. It also attacked symbols of U.S. "imperialism," including U.S. banks, corporations, agencies, and citizens; took over churches during religious services, as in Arequipa on March 4, 1987; and undertook car bombings and kidnappings.

A rural foco was established in late 1987 in Juanjui, located in the department of San Martín. One of the last major actions of the group was the kidnapping of Raúl Hiraoka, the son of the founder of a major Peruvian appliance chain.

The MRTA's main leader, Víctor Polay, was captured in June 1992 and is serving life in prison, as is his lieutenant, Peter Cárdenas. The group virtually dissolved on July 12, 1993, when other top commanders surrendered and urged diehard members to do the same.

PARTIDO COMUNISTA DEL PERU POR EL SENDERO LUMINOSO DEL PENSAMIENTO DE JOSE CARLOS MARIATEGUI
Communist Party of Peru Through the Shining Path of the Thought of José Carlos Mariátegui

Initiated guerrilla activity in 1980; Maoist-Mariateguista; operated initially in the Peruvian Andes and then in urban areas; maximum strength estimated at between 10,000 and 12,000; led by Abimael Guzmán (aka "Comrade Gonzalo," captured on September 12, 1992), Luis Kawata Mackabe, Osmán Morote, Julio Casanova, Catalina Adrianzen, and Antonio Díaz Martínez; represented by the front organization Movimiento Obreros, Trabajadores y Campesinos (MOTC, Movement of Workers, Working People and Peasants).

The origins of Sendero Luminoso can be traced back to the early 1960s in the rural city of Huamanga, capital of the Peruvian department of Ayacucho, where an organization known as the Huamanga Command of the Ejército de Liberación Nacional was active within the National University of San Cristóbal de Huamanga.

Abimael Guzmán, a professor hired in 1963, quickly became the leader of the Huamanga Command. Over the next couple of years he built up his power base, recruiting students for trips to Cuba and for participation in local literacy, farming, and nutrition assistance programs. Guzmán, who earned his doctorate in philosophy in the city of Arequipa, filtered Maoist thought through the prism of Peruvian intellectual José Carlos Mariátegui, founder of the Partido Comunista del Perú.

A member of the PCP since the 1950s, in 1966 Guzmán sided with the Partido Comunista del Perú—Bandera Roja (PCP-BR, Communist Party of Peru—Red Flag), the Maoist breakaway faction of the pro-Soviet Peruvian Communist Party. However, he and his followers either withdrew or were expelled from the party over doctrinal differences in 1968. By 1970, this faction had become the Partido Comunista del Perú por el Sendero Luminoso del Pensamiento de José Carlos Mariátegui, or Sendero Luminoso.

During the 1970s, Sendero refined and solidified its ideology. Echoing Mao and Mariátegui, the movement maintained that imperialism in Peru created a dependent capitalist economy that lacked a dominant capitalist class because the Peruvian state had abdicated in favor of foreign capital.

As its primary support base, Sendero not only targeted the impoverished Peruvian peasantry but also, beginning in the 1980s, disenfranchised urban dwellers. The military government of this period unwittingly played into the movement's hands by promoting largely ineffective rural programs. The much-heralded agrarian reform of the Velazco Alvarado regime was unsuccessful in Ayacucho, and the government officials sent to the area characteristically did not speak Quechua, were paid low wages, and had virtually no infrastructural support for their activities. These conditions facilitated the growth of Sendero's influence in the area. Members of the movement provided paramedical, farming, and literacy services and also married into peasant families. The movement intended to introduce a socialist dictatorship of the proletariat in Peru, a goal that would call upon Peruvians to do more than simply make a few systemic adjustments to benefit the marginalized sectors of the country; rather, they would have to reject all the forms of government that the country had experienced since Incan times.

Between March and May 1980, Sendero's Central Committee intensified its preparation for armed conflict through a series of meetings. Notes

from these meetings show the extremely high level of ideological motivation employed by Guzmán in preparing his cohorts for the rebellion.
The bulk of time in the initial meetings was spent not on military tactics
but on methodological reflections on the interrelationships between
Maoist theory and praxis.

The Sendero hierarchy considered the 1980s a "critical decade" for the
insurrection. In the movement's phases of growth, Sendero would first
adopt a posture of "strategic defense" in which guerrilla warfare would
dominate its actions. "Strategic equilibrium" would occur once the
movement was strong enough to withstand direct attacks from the
armed forces, which Guzmán realized would inevitably enter the conflict. These two phases were planned to roughly correspond with Peru's
presidential periods (1980–1985, 1985–1990). From there, Sendero would
move to a "strategic offensive" that would bring about the final victory.
The group was uncertain how long this final period would take, but
Guzmán would go through with it all "even if it took 75 years."

Sendero launched its armed struggle on May 17, 1980, one day before
Peru's general elections, when five insurgents broke into an electoral
registration office in the rural town of Chuschi in Ayacucho and burned
the ballot boxes. Neither the local nor the national press took much note
of the incident. During the remainder of 1980 and through 1981, Sendero
attacks included the bombing of public buildings and private businesses.
Still, the growing insurgency in Ayacucho seemed too isolated and far
removed for the excessively centralized Lima government to take interest. President Fernando Belaúnde Terry's government officials often
dismissed Sendero Luminoso as a group of "common delinquents" or
"cattle thieves." By 1982, Sendero's actions had escalated to assassinations of local public figures in the Ayacucho area, and the area police
were placed in charge of the investigations. The first time that the major
national media actually took notice of Sendero was in March of that year,
when the guerrillas staged a massive raid and jailbreak from the main
Ayacucho prison. At this point, Peruvians had become very concerned
about the group's violent activities.

The first Sendero action in Lima took place on June 16, 1982, when
some 200 youths attacked a municipal building in the San Martín de Po-
rres district. Although Sendero's philosophy mandated that it concentrate on the countryside and the peasantry as its battleground and support base, respectively, there were many months between 1982 and 1987

in which Sendero attacks in Lima exceeded those in Ayacucho. However, Guzmán never ceased to consider the countryside as the movement's strategic focus, for both the accumulation of forces and the location of the final battle.

Between 1980 and 1982, Sendero overwhelmed the police in Ayacucho, forcing the January 1983 entrance of the armed forces into the conflict after Belaúnde Terry declared a state of emergency in Ayacucho. More than 5,000 people, mainly civilians, died in 1983 and 1984 as the conflict escalated. Sendero was not only able to survive during these years but even managed to open new fronts, such as those in the country's central Andean region as well as in the Huallaga valley. These developments contributed to increased confidence among Sendero's ranks.

In 1988, the movement held its First National Congress, which included discussions of the progress made throughout the decade and stressed the upcoming transition to "strategic equilibrium." This transition entailed a movement from guerrilla warfare to open combat. Sendero thus required additional combatants and better weapons and, more important, needed the active support of the population, not simply the passive consent that it had formerly enjoyed among some elements. But this process was made increasingly difficult because of the emergence of civilian, government-supported "self-defense militias" in the countryside. This obstacle led Sendero to again concentrate its efforts in Lima, where it attempted to recruit new members from the poverty-stricken shantytowns. Sendero was relatively successful in this effort because, in contrast to the seemingly indifferent central government, the movement represented what appeared to be a viable alternative for the disenfranchised and isolated population, a large portion of which had been displaced by the internal war itself.

By 1990, approximately one-third of Peru's territory and half of its population was under military control. Also, hyperinflation had reached 60 percent monthly. These uncertain conditions contributed to the populace's growing discontent and to the election of outsider Alberto Fujimori to the presidency that year. For the first time in its counterinsurgency activities, the army had a civilian leader willing to meaningfully confront the guerrillas, even if this required shifting away from the country's institutional democracy. Fujimori's April 1992 *autogolpe,* in which he dissolved Congress and revamped the judiciary, began this shift. In the months following the breakdown of constitutional rule, Fujimori's authoritarian regime issued several insurgency-related supreme decrees that the legislature had previously attempted to modify. Meanwhile, the military counterinsurgency campaign intensified.

On July 16, a Sendero van bomb detonated on Tarata Street in Miraflores, a residential Lima neighborhood. Twenty-five people were killed and thousands injured. This attack, in conjunction with Sendero's widely obeyed "armed strike" of July 22–23, created a state of desperation and resignation in the country. National and international observers began to regard Peru as irretrievably in the hands of Sendero. The "new offensive" against Lima, scheduled for October or November, had the city in a state of paralysis. It appeared that Sendero's goal of "strategic equilibrium"—making the country impossible to govern—would soon be achieved.

But on September 12, Guzmán was captured in an upper middle-class Lima neighborhood by DINCOTE, a special police antiterrorist unit. His arrest was a devastating blow to the movement, which had come to view Guzmán as almost a godlike figure. The event was even more crucial because an important attack against Lima authorities, devised by Guzmán and to be carried out under his supervision, had been planned for just a few weeks after the arrest.

Several of Sendero Luminoso's top leaders were captured along with Guzmán. In addition, important documents, including Sendero's "New State in Construction" archives, which laid out the movement's plans, as well as the names of many of the organization's members, fell into the hands of the authorities.

These developments profoundly shook Sendero and put it back on the defensive. After the capture, the group's attacks noticeably decreased. Estimates put the total number of active guerrillas at merely 1,500, although they still control Raucana, a community of 60,000. For the first time, however, the government holds a tactical advantage in the war. Fujimori may very well be able to fulfill his promise to completely defeat the guerrillas in the future.

Bibliographical Commentary

João Batista Berardo's *Guerrilhas e guerrilheiros no drama da América Latina* is often confusing but offers good corroborative data. For accounts of the saga of Hugo Blanco and Luis de la Puente Uceda's Movimiento de Izquierda Revolucionaria, consult Richard Gott's comprehensive *Guerrilla Movements in Latin America*. Alain Gandolfi, in *Les luttes armées en*

Amerique Latine, offers details about Héctor Béjar's Ejército de Liberación Nacional. Donald Hodges objectively discusses Blanco's and de la Puente Uceda's theories and strategies in *The Latin American Revolution: Politics and Strategy from Apro-Marxism to Guevarism.* The development of the most recent (and bloodiest) Peruvian insurgent movement, the Shining Path, has been well covered by both scholars and the popular press. For the quickest overview of the movement, there's Alma Guillermoprieto's "Down the Shining Path," a lengthy feature that ran in *The New Yorker* and frames the history of the movement through a profile of its leader, Abimael Guzmán. For a more in-depth view, consult *From the Sierras to the Cities: The Urban Campaign of the Shining Path,* by Gordon McCormick. *Latin American Revolutionaries: Groups, Goals, Methods,* by Michael Radu and Vladimir Tismaneanu, can be used to corroborate data and for information about smaller groups.

18

URUGUAY

MOVIMIENTO DE LIBERACION NACIONAL TUPAMAROS
Movement of National Liberation-Tupamaros

Active from 1962 to 1972, when it was destroyed by the army; Marxist; its best known operation was the kidnapping of U.S. official Dan Mitrione; operated mainly in Montevideo and other small cities and towns in Uruguay; led by Raúl Sendic, Abraham Guillén, and Pedro Almirati; largely self-financed.

The Movimiento de Liberación Nacional Tupamaros was formed as an extension of a 1961 protest in which Raúl Sendic, a thirty-six-year-old law student from Montevideo, led a group of poverty-stricken sugar farmers in their demands for higher pay and decent working conditions. Soon their ideology deviated from these social demands and they began to call for land expropriation and income redistribution. After spending time in prison for his role in the protest, Sendic and a group of friends concluded that the traditional political system was not equipped to channel their demands. To them, the legal means of political participation had become useless. They founded the Tupamaros to bring about a new system in which the interests of all Uruguayans would be represented.

The guerrilla group emerged from what many considered an unlikely foundation for a popular revolt. However, Uruguay's intrinsic qualities led to the formation of a new type of revolutionary association—one that utilized the predominantly urban makeup of the country to its advantage. Although the nation's population reached only about 2.5 million at the time of the group's formation, almost 80 percent of it was concentrated in the cities.

When this highly urbanized society was hit with an economic crisis in 1954, rural and urban workers bore the brunt. The Tupamaros vowed to take up an armed struggle in order to create an independent nationalist identity and implement socialism as Uruguay's socioeconomic system.

The revolutionaries believed that violence was both the justifiable right of a people who wished to revolt against their government and the most effective method of seizing power in the nation. Their first major action came in July 1963, when a group of guerrillas raided a Swiss rifle club in order to augment its reserves of weaponry. Later that year, the Tupamaros attacked a delivery truck carrying chickens and turkeys destined for a Christmas eve banquet and later distributed the food to the residents of a destitute neighborhood. The movement was largely financed through robberies of private and government-owned banks, casinos, and wealthy citizens. In 1970, a group of guerrillas stole about $6 million in jewelry from a private mansion in Montevideo—the largest jewel robbery in recent history.

The Tupamaros carried out some notable military actions during their years of operation and succeeded in garnering a fairly large amount of popular support. By the late 1960s, the name of the group was well recognized and respected among students, trade unionists, and left-wing political parties.

Two branches of the National Police were assigned the task of combatting the group: the Metropolitan Guard and the Intelligence Directorate, both well supplied and trained by the U.S. AID Office of Public Safety. Although the guerrillas decried the climate of repression and the frequent use of torture by the police, it was the army that ultimately played a key role in the rebels' defeat.

The ascent in 1967 of Vice President Jorge Pacheco Areco to the presidency marked the beginning of a period of harsh repression of the population. The new leader faced an economic fiasco, strikes, student unrest, and a violent revolutionary faction. Pacheco proceeded to ban six minor leftist political parties because of their alleged support of armed struggle. In addition, the police were placed under military rule and the code of justice. Despite increased control over the public, however, the guerrillas struck back in 1969 with a huge offensive, kidnapping banker G. Pelligrini Gianpietro on September 9 and seizing the town of Pando, about 20 miles south of the capital, for a few hours on October 8, in commemoration of Che Guevara's death, to demonstrate the extent of their power. Gianpietro was released on November 21 after payment of ransom.

In 1970, the Tupamaros succeeded in abducting Dan Mitrione, the U.S. AID official who had trained the police in the harsh interrogation of political prisoners. In response, Pacheco tightened control by ordering house-to-house searches and censoring the press in an effort to eliminate the word "Tupamaro" from the national vocabulary. Newspaper closures, both temporary and permanent, became routine.

Propaganda had become a key part of the guerrillas' strategy during this era of the conflict. Before the imposition of censorship, the rebels had sent letters to Uruguayan newspapers and had issued communiqués through the mass media and granted interviews to reporters. In addition, it was common practice to seize cinemas, factories, and other businesses in order to disseminate statements to entranced audiences. The movement also ensured that its abductions and other actions—especially its "Robin Hood" propaganda schemes in which food was stolen and doled out among Uruguay's poor—were highly publicized.

These actions bolstered their increasing support within the country. Popular demonstrations composed of students and trade unionists highlighted the Tupamaros' relatively high standing in Uruguayan society. Their hold in the universities was secure owing to intense propaganda and a burgeoning underground movement. Labor unions were also hotbeds of support before their activities were severely curtailed by the government. Committees in support of the Tupamaros were formed in many businesses, and the movement also sought to establish ties with leftist political parties within Uruguay as well as armed movements abroad. In 1970, the Tupamaros held a roundtable that brought together guerrilla movements of the continent. The notion of a continental strategy with a single unified command was rejected, but the participants did agree to coordinate actions in the Southern Cone, Bolivia, and Brazil.

During this period of ideological consolidation, the guerrillas strengthened their political ties within Uruguay. They decided to call a temporary truce in observance of the 1971 elections and, instead of acting on their advantage, supported the nascent leftist coalition Frente Amplio (Broad Front), a party of Socialists, Communists, Christian Democrats, and dissident factions of the Colorados and Blancos that had become a serious electoral contender. Some analysts, in retrospect, deem this move as a crucial mistake, contending that the guerrillas did not take advantage of their strong position in the battle with the government at this time. Outside of Uruguay, the Tupamaros kept in contact with political movements driven by nationalism and socialism rather than by revolutionary fervor. The rebels closely followed Salvador Allende's triumph in Chile as well as events in Peru, Ecuador, and Bolivia.

The years 1971–1972 marked a period of upheaval for the Tupamaros, the Uruguayan military, and the nation itself. The armed forces were given carte blanche in their dealings with the guerrilla movement. A month after Pacheco was succeeded by Juan M. Bordaberry, the revolutionary organization carried out what was to be its last series of attacks. In early 1971, the guerrillas abducted British ambassador G. Jackson and launched a general offensive that included five other kidnappings as well as a dozen major robberies. During this time, the revolutionaries virtually ran a parallel government and generated increasing support among the people.

These years were also characterized by the formation of both leftist and rightist groups in this atmosphere of revolutionary chaos. Smaller urban guerrilla groups—such as the Organización Popular Revolucionaria–33 (OPR-33, Popular Revolutionary Organization–33) and the Fuerzas Armadas Revolucionarias Orientales (FARO, Oriental Revolutionary Armed Forces)—were sometimes founded by disgruntled Tupamaros who disagreed with the movement's strategies and goals, but they never carried any significant influence. On the other end of the political spectrum, several ultraright groups came into existence in order to break the Tupamaros' stranglehold on the nation. Organizations such as the Juventud Uruguaya de Pie (JUP, Uruguayan Youth at Attention) and the Comando Caza Tupamaros (Tupamaros Hunt Commando), allegedly created and financially supported by government and law-enforcement authorities, harassed families of suspected guerrillas and assassinated known members. A number of high schools even closed down as student violence reached its peak in June 1971.

The armed forces played a key role in eliminating the Tupamaros. Up until then considered one of the most apolitical armies in the hemisphere, the Uruguayan military was thrust onto the scene as the president invited it into the fray once the National Police proved ineffective. Extremely helpful to the military was the inside information provided by H. Amodio Pérez, a captured guerrilla leader. The military carried out its objective by obtaining from the new president the *Ley de Seguridad del Estado* (Law of Security of the State), a declaration of internal war that allowed it to detain leftist sympathizers indiscriminately, regulate the press, and ban political parties while implementing a system of harsh interrogation and torture. The military also succeeded in removing the Tupamaros' influence from smaller cities and rural areas.

By mid-1972, the guerrilla influence within the nation had been essentially eliminated and the armed forces were anxious to establish national security and rid the government of endemic corruption. On June 27, 1973, the military took power in a deal with the president whereby Bordaberry was allowed to remain in office in exchange for most of his constitutional power. During this period, the president was allowed to reign, but the military ruled.

Bibliographical Commentary

Bibliography on the Tupamaros, the first group ever to sustain a foco in an urban environment, is plentiful and of generally high caliber. In addition to works devoted exclusively to the movement, like the classic *The Tupamaro Guerrillas*, by María Esther Gilio, or Carlos Wilson's *The Tupamaros, the Unmentionables*, there are numerous references to the movement included in more general works. James Kohl devotes a section to the Tupamaros in his *Urban Guerrilla Warfare in Latin America* and mentions lesser groups. *Uruguay in Transition*, by Edy Kaufman, includes passages on the dynamic between the Tupamaros and military organizations.

19

VENEZUELA

MOVIMIENTO DE IZQUIERDA REVOLUCIONARIA/FUERZAS ARMADAS DE LIBERACION NACIONAL (MIR-FALN)
Movement of the Revolutionary Left/
Armed Forces of National Liberation

Active from 1960 to late 1960s; led by Domingo Alberto Rangel, Moisés Moleiro, and Américo Martín; Castrist; represented by the legal organization Frente de Liberación Nacional (FLN, National Liberation Front).

The popular revolution that deposed dictator Marcos Pérez Jiménez in early 1958 brought Rómulo Betancourt of Acción Democrática (AD, Democratic Action) to power. AD, once the largest and most progressive party in Venezuela, had by that time lost its youthful enthusiasm for reform and was pursuing a reactionary line, and Venezuelan guerrillas derived support from those who felt betrayed by this turn of events.

Domingo Alberto Rangel and Simón Saez Mérida were among the radical elements of AD. On April 9, 1960, in a conference in Maracaibo, Rangel and journalist Américo Martín founded the Acción Democrática Izquierdista (Leftist Democratic Action), which later changed its name to Movimiento de Izquierda Revolucionaria. This radicalized wing of the AD was the first organization to engage in armed struggle in Venezuela.

On October 20, six MIR members were detained on charges of subversion. The arrests were followed by protests that left six dead and about 500 taken into custody. The disturbances continued through November and December, but the army eventually crushed them.

The year 1962 saw the first outbreaks of guerrilla warfare, and the government issued a decree on May 10 outlawing the MIR as well as the Communist Party.

In Caracas in 1963 the MIR, along with Communists and disaffected military officers, set up the Fuerzas Armadas de Liberación Nacional. The FALN, formally established at a meeting held in Caracas in February 1963, consisted of some 500 guerrillas organized into five brigades, two controlled by the MIR and three by the Communist Party. Each brigade required logistical support from an additional 300 to 400 personnel and was organized internally into teams of five to six men. These teams carried out arsons, murders, robberies, acts of sabotage, and other forms of violence. The FALN's political branch was the Frente de Liberación Nacional, established on July 4, 1964.

The elections of December 1, 1963, brought the AD's Raúl Leoni to power. Leoni announced a national reconciliation, forcing the guerrillas to reassess their position. Eventually, in 1964, Rangel came out in favor of peaceful struggle. His letter, written from prison, caused a crisis within the MIR and Rangel's replacement by Saez Mérida.

The Partido Bandera Roja, a group from the MIR that wanted to persist in the armed struggle, was active briefly in 1969 and operated in Venezuela and eastern Colombia under the leadership of Gabriel Puerta Aponte and Asdrúbal Cordero.

PARTIDO COMUNISTA DE VENEZUELA/
FUERZAS ARMADAS DE LIBERACION NACIONAL (PCV-FALN)
Communist Party of Venezuela/
Armed Forces of National Liberation

Active from 1961 to 1968; led by Douglas Bravo; represented by the legal organization Frente de Liberación Nacional.

The Partido Comunista de Venezuela was the second major political group after the Movimiento de Izquierda Revolucionaria to join the guerrilla struggle in the South American nation.

Following the riots of October through December 1961, President Rómulo Betancourt cracked down on Communist leaders, convinced that they had played a major role in the disturbances. Several leaders were found guilty of subversion, and the PCV drifted toward armed opposition to the government. In its Third Party Congress of January 1961, the leadership voted to adopt a party line of nonpeaceful development of the revolutionary struggle in Venezuela.

In the meantime, Douglas Bravo and other PCV members secretly organized logistical support for rural guerrilla operations in the eastern and western mountains. These began early in 1962, although the army quickly tracked them down and broke up their operations.

Betancourt's government was besieged by revolutionaries that year. Within the cities, urban guerrillas—largely university students from the PCV and the MIR—organized themselves into Unidades Tácticas de Combate (Tactical Combat Units) and carried out a terrorist campaign of arson, assassination, and robbery. In rural areas, PCV-led peasants were also active.

To make matters worse, naval captain Jesús Teodoro Molina, supported by 450 marines, captured the naval base at Carúpano (250 miles from Caracas) on May 2, 1962. The rebellion was contained in two days, but Betancourt was angered by the PCV's support of the rebels. On May 10, the president outlawed the PCV and initiated an all-out search for Communist Party leaders.

The guerrillas also tried to assassinate Betancourt during his visit to Ciudad Bolívar on June 12, 1962. They failed in the attempt, but the incident prompted the president to intensify his pursuit of Communists. Betancourt was helped in this campaign by a guerrilla attack on an excursion train at El Encanto in September, which killed five members of the National Guard. On October 1, Congress lifted parliamentary immunity to the PCV and the MIR, and a number of legislators were arrested in the following weeks.

Early in 1962, Bravo had fled to his native state of Falcón, on the Caribbean coast between Caracas and Maracaibo, where he founded what would later become the first guerrilla division of the Fuerzas Armadas de Liberación Nacional.

But the failure of the rural and urban campaigns forced the guerrillas to reassess their strategy by the end of the year. The PCV, in its December plenum, voted to adopt a policy of all-out struggle against Betancourt. On February 20, 1963, at a meeting in Caracas, the PCV formally joined with the MIR, military deserters, and other disaffected groups to create the FALN.

With the presidential elections set for December 1, 1963, the guerrillas intended to create a climate of terror that would bring down Betancourt and civilian rule. Then, they hoped to rally support from politically disaffected groups, topple the military that had ousted Betancourt, and gain control of the government.

To this end, they adopted the slogan "kill a policeman a day" and took advantage of discontent in the city slums or *ranchos,* using them or the Central University as safe havens following attacks on police stations, banks, and other targets. They also bombed and burned oil installations, factories, and stores—mainly those owned by U.S. interests—and engaged in attention-getting stunts, such as the seizure of valuable items from a touring exhibition of French art and the kidnapping of an Argentine soccer star.

On November 10, the FALN issued a communiqué urging people not to participate in the elections because the electoral path was not the solution for Venezuela. The group also tried to cancel the election by calling for a general strike on November 19. FALN guerrillas paralyzed Caracas for two days, but most unions did not join in the work stoppage. On November 28, three tons of arms and ammunition were discovered on the Paraguana peninsula. Betancourt took advantage of this episode to point out to the electorate how Cuban leader Fidel Castro was trying to interfere in Venezuela's internal affairs and promote the guerrillas.

Raúl Leoni, the AD candidate supported by Betancourt, won. This election was a watershed event for the guerrillas, who later admitted that they had concentrated on urban action in the hopes of a quick victory.

In April 1964, at the PCV's Sixth Party Congress, the Central Committee decided to abandon urban sabotage in favor of a long-term rural guerrilla campaign. The cadres saw four stages in the new approach: the intensification of terrorism, which PCV leaders felt had been completed in 1963; the intensification of guerrilla warfare in certain areas of the country; true civil war against the army; and opposition against the U.S. forces that would surely be sent in.

The army, however, successfully counterattacked in 1964 and 1965. Even though guerrilla warfare, such as attacks on police and sabotage of oil pipes, continued, the movement was never again able to pose a serious threat to the government. In the ideological arena, during these years the groups making up the FALN split over the issue of the use of violence. Although some advocated peaceful means, others supported the idea of continuing the use of violence for some time.

By 1966, the Communist leadership was persuaded that the time had come to abandon armed struggle for an accommodation with the government in line with Leoni's promise to legalize the party if it renounced the use of violence. Thereafter, most PCV leaders gradually withdrew from the revolutionary program of violent attacks in order to participate in the 1968 elections behind the facade of a shadow party known as the Unión para Progreso (Union for Progress).

Douglas Bravo, however, furiously denounced the change in direction. In January 1966 he published a letter in which he denounced the new pacifist tendencies of the PCV. Two months later, he made known his political aspirations in his *Manifesto de Iracara* (Valsalice 1979: 81), in which he stated that armed struggle should never be suspended. Supported by Havana, guerrilla activities continued in the mountains of the east and northwest, with sporadic raids occurring through 1968. The militants, who made an unsuccessful attempt to intimidate potential voters into boycotting the presidential elections of 1968, were dealt a mortal blow in 1969, when Castro cut off aid to guerrillas as a first step in a five-year campaign to resume relations with Venezuela. Some guerrilla bands managed to survive in isolated regions for a few years but posed no real danger to the government.

Bibliographical Commentary

Luigi Valsalice's *La guerrilla castrista en Venezuela y sus protagonistas, 1962–1969* is an extremely detailed account of the activities of Douglas Bravo and the Communist Party of Venezuela. For a quick overview, consult Raymond Estep's brief but well-organized account in *Guerrilla Warfare in Latin America, 1963–1975*. Vania Bambirra, Alvaro Lopez, Moisés Moleiro, Silvestre Condoruma, Carlos Nuñez, Ruy Mauro Marini, and Antonio Zapata, in *Diez años de insurrección en América Latina*, approach the topic from a decidedly leftist standpoint, giving preference to analysis rather than raw data. For two more balanced accounts of the Venezuelan experience, consult Luis Mercier Vega's *Guerrillas in Latin America: The Technique of Counter-State* and Robert Moss's *Urban Guerrillas*.

Bibliography

BOOKS

General

Bambirra, Vania, Alvaro Lopez, Moisés Moleiro, Silvestre Condoruma, Carlos Nuñez, Ruy Mauro Marini, and Antonio Zapata. *Diez años de insurrección en América Latina*. Santiago, Chile: Editorial Prensa Latinoamericana, 1971.

Berardo, João Batista. *Guerrilhas e guerrilheiros no drama da América Latina*. Coleçao América Latina, Serie Nossa Historia, Nossos Problemas. São Paulo, Brazil: Ediciones Populares, 1981.

Burbach, Roger, and Orlando Nuñez. *Fire in the Americas: Forging a Revolutionary Agenda*. New York: Verso, 1987.

Carr, Barry, and Steve Ellner, eds. *The Latin American Left from the Fall of Allende to Perestroika*. Boulder: Westview Press, 1993.

Castañeda, Jorge. *Utopia Unarmed: The Latin American Left After the Cold War*. New York: Knopf, 1993.

Degenhardt, Henry W. *Political Dissent: An International Guide to Dissident, Extra-Parliamentary, Guerrilla and Illegal Political Movements*. Burnt Mill, Eng.: Longman House, 1983.

_____, ed. *Revolutionary and Dissident Movements: An International Guide*. Harlow, Essex, Eng.: Longman; Detroit, Mich.: Gale Research, 1988.

Estep, Raymond. *Guerrilla Warfare in Latin America, 1963–1975*. Maxwell Air Force Base, Ala.: Directorate of Documentary Research, Air University Institute for Professional Development, 1975.

Fauriol, Georges. *Latin American Insurgencies*. Washington, D.C.: Georgetown University Center for Strategic and International Studies/National Defense University, 1985.

Gandolfi, Alain. *Les luttes armées en Amerique Latine*. Paris, France: Presses Universitaires de France, 1991.

Gott, Richard. *Guerrilla Movements in Latin America*. Garden City, N.Y.: Anchor Books, 1972.

_____. *Rural Guerrillas in Latin America*. Harmondsworth, Eng.: Penguin Books, 1973.

Gunson, Phil, Greg Chamberlain, and Andres Thompson, eds. *The Dictionary of*

Contemporary Politics of Central America and the Caribbean. New York: Simon and Schuster, 1991.

Hodges, Donald C. *The Latin American Revolution: Politics and Strategy from Apro-Marxism to Guevarism.* New York: William Morrow, 1974.

Hopkins, Jack W., ed. *Latin American and Caribbean Contemporary Record, Vol. 2, 1982–1983.* New York: Holmes & Meier, 1984.

Jonas, Susanne, and Nancy Stein, eds. *Democracy in Latin America: Visions and Realities.* New York: Bergin and Garvey, 1990.

Kohl, James. *Urban Guerrilla Warfare in Latin America.* Cambridge: MIT Press, 1974.

Mercier Vega, Luis. Translated by Daniel Weissbort. *Guerrillas in Latin America: The Technique of the Counter-State.* New York: Praeger, 1969.

Moss, Robert. *Revolution in Latin America.* London, Eng.: The Economist Newspaper Ltd., 1971.

_____. *Urban Guerrillas.* London, Eng.: Temple Smith, 1970.

Radu, Michael, and Vladimir Tismaneanu. *Latin American Revolutionaries: Groups, Goals, Methods.* Washington, D.C.: Pergamon Brassey International Defense Publishers, 1990.

Rossi, Ernest E., and Jack C. Plano. *Latin America: A Political Dictionary.* Santa Barbara, Calif.: ABC-CLIO, 1992.

Wickham-Crowley, Timothy. *Guerrillas and Revolution in Latin America: A Comparative Study of Insurgents and Regimes Since 1956.* Princeton, N.J.: Princeton University Press, 1992.

Argentina

Andersen, Martin. *Dossier Secreto: Argentina's Desaparecidos and the Myth of the 'Dirty War.'* Boulder: Westview Press, 1993.

Anzorena, Oscar R. *Tiempo de violencia y utopia.* Buenos Aires: Ediciones Contrapunto, 1988.

Di Tella, Guido. *Argentina Under Perón (1973–1976): The Nation's Experience with a Labour-based Government.* New York: St. Martin's Press, 1983.

Gillespie, Richard. *Soldiers of Perón: Argentina's Montoneros.* New York: Clarendon Press, 1982.

Giussani, Pablo. *Montoneros: La soberbia armada.* Buenos Aires: Ediciones Sudamericana Planeta, 1984.

Graziano, Frank. *Divine Violence: Spectacle, Psychosexuality, and Radical Christianity in the Argentine 'Dirty War.'* Boulder: Westview Press, 1992.

Hodges, Donald C. *Argentina, 1943–1976: The National Revolution and Resistance.* Albuquerque: University of New Mexico Press, 1976.

_____. *Argentina's 'Dirty War': An Intellectual Biography.* Austin: University of Texas Press, 1991.

Méndez, Eugenio. *Confesiones de un Montonero.* Buenos Aires: Ediciones Sudamericana Planeta, 1985.

Seoane, Maria. *Todo o nada*. Buenos Aires: Ediciones Planeta, Espejo de la Argentina, 1991.

Bolivia

Debray, Régis. *Defensa en Camiri*. Montevideo: Siglo Ilustrado, 1968.

Harris, Richard. *Death of a Revolutionary: Che Guevara's Last Mission*. New York: W. W. Norton, 1970.

Prado Salmón, Gary. *The Defeat of Che Guevara: Military Response to Guerrilla Challenge in Bolivia*. New York: Praeger, 1990.

Weil, Thomas E., Jan Knippers Black, Howard I. Blutstein, Hans J. Hoyer, Kathryn T. Johnston, and David S. McMorris. *Area Handbook for Bolivia*. Foreign Area Studies Series. Washington, D.C.: The American University, 1974.

Brazil

Burns, E. Bradford. *A History of Brazil*. New York: Columbia University Press, 1993.

Mallin, Jay, ed. *Terror and Urban Guerrillas: A Study of Tactics and Documents*. Coral Gables, Fla.: University of Miami Press, 1971.

Marighella, Carlos. *Minimanual of the Urban Guerrilla*. Washington, D.C.: Joint Publications Research Service, 1970.

Chile

Alexander, Robert J. *The Tragedy of Chile*. Westport, Conn.: Greenwood Press, 1987.

Bizzarro, Salvatore. *Historical Dictionary of Chile*, 2nd ed. Metuchen, N.J.: Scarecrow Press, 1987.

Constable, Pamela, and Arturo Valenzuela. *A Nation of Enemies: Chile Under Pinochet*. New York: W. W. Norton, 1991.

Drake, Paul W., and Ivan Jaksik, eds. *The Struggle for Democracy in Chile, 1982–1990*. Lincoln: University of Nebraska Press, 1991.

Furci, Carmelo. *The Chilean Communist Party and the Road to Socialism*. London, Eng.: Zed Books, Ltd., 1984.

Whelan, James R. *Out of the Ashes: Life, Death and Transfiguration of Democracy in Chile, 1933–1988*. Washington, D.C.: Regenery Gateway, 1989.

Colombia

Arrubla, Mario, Jésus Antonio Bejarano, J. G. Cobo Borda, Jaime Jaramillo Uribe, Salomón Kalamanowitz, Jorge Orlando Melo, and Alvaro Tirado Mejía. *Colombia, hoy*, 11th ed. Bogotá, Col.: Siglo XXI Editores de Colombia, 1987; first published in 1978.

Bushnell, David. *The Making of Modern Colombia*. Berkeley: University of California Press, 1993.

Colombia: A Country Study. Area Handbook Series. Washington, D.C.: Department of the Army, 1990.

Colombia: Violencia y democracia. Bogotá, Col.: Universidad Nacional de Colombia, Centro Editorial, 1987.

En que momento se jodió Colombia. Bogotá, Col.: Editorial La Oveja Negra Limitada, 1990; Lima, Peru: Coedición Editorial Milla Batres, 1990.

Maullin, Richard L. *Soldiers, Guerrillas and Politics in Colombia.* Lexington, Mass.: Lexington Books, 1973.

Pearce, Jenny. *Colombia: Inside the Labyrinth.* London, Eng.: Latin American Bureau (Research and Action) Ltd., 1990.

Rodríguez Gómez, Héctor Mario, ed. *Almanaque Colombia, 1993.* Bogotá, Col.: Ediciones El Carnero, 1993.

Sánchez G., Gonzalo, and Donny Meertens. *Bandoleros, gamonales y campesinos: El caso de la violencia en Colombia.* Bogotá, Col.: El Ancora Editores, 1983.

Cuba

Bonachea, Rolando, ed. Compiled by Rolando Bonachea and Nelson P. Valdés. *Cuba in Revolution.* Garden City, N.Y.: Anchor Books, 1972.

Brenner, Philip, William M. LeoGrande, Donna Rich, and Daniel Siegel, eds. *The Cuba Reader: The Making of a Revolutionary Society.* New York: Grove Press, 1989.

Castro, Fidel. *La historia me absolverá.* Spain: Ediciones Júcar, 1976.

———. *Revolutionary Struggle, 1947–1958.* Cambridge: MIT Press, 1972.

Karol, K. S. Translated by Arnold Pomerans. *Guerrillas in Power: The Course of the Cuban Revolution.* New York: Hill & Wang, 1970.

Liss, Sheldon B. *Roots of Revolution: Radical Thought in Cuba.* Lincoln: University of Nebraska Press, 1987.

Rudolph, James D., ed. *Cuba: A Country Study.* Foreign Area Studies, The American University. Washington, D.C.: Department of the Army, 1985.

Dominican Republic

Raful, Tony. *Movimiento 14 de junio: historia y documentos.* Santo Domingo, República Dominicana: Editora Alfa & Omega, 1983.

El Salvador

Armstrong, Robert, and Janet Shenk. *El Salvador: The Face of Revolution.* Boston: South End Press, 1982.

Barry, Tom. *El Salvador: A Country Guide.* Albuquerque: Inter-Hemispheric Education Resource Center, 1990.

Haggerty, Richard A., ed. *El Salvador: A Country Study.* U.S. Government, Federal Research Divison, 1990.

Montgomery, Tommie Sue. *Revolution in El Salvador: Origins and Evolution.* Boulder: Westview Press, 1982.

North, Liisa. Bitter Grounds: Roots of Revolt in El Salvador. Toronto, Canada: Between the Lines, 1985.

Prisk, Courtney E., ed. The Comandante Speaks. Boulder: Westview Press, 1991.

Tulchin, Joseph S., ed., with Gary Bland. Is There a Transition to Democracy in El Salvador? Boulder: Lynne Rienner, Inc., 1992.

Grenada

Dujmovic, Nicholas. The Grenada Documents: Window on Totalitarianism. Cambridge, Mass.: Institute for Foreign Policy Analysis; Washington, D.C.: Pergamon Brassey International Defense Publishers, 1988.

Sandford, Gregory. The New Jewel Movement: Grenada's Revolution, 1979–1983. Washington, D.C.: Center for the Study of Foreign Affairs, Foreign Service Institute, U.S. Department of State, 1985.

Guatemala

Barry, Tom. Inside Guatemala. Albuquerque: Inter-Hemispheric Education Resource Center, 1992.

Bouchey, L. Francis, and Alberto M. Piedra. Guatemala: A Promise in Peril. Washington, D.C.: Council for Inter-American Security, 1980.

Handy, Jim. Gift of the Devil. Boston: South End Press, 1984.

Jonas, Susanne. The Battle for Guatemala: Rebels, Death Squads and U.S. Power. Boulder: Westview Press, 1991.

Honduras

Acker, Alison. Honduras: The Making of a Banana Republic. Boston: South End Press, 1988.

Rudolph, James D., ed. Honduras: A Country Study. Foreign Area Studies. Washington, D.C.: The American University, 1983.

Nicaragua

Gilbert, Dennis. Sandinistas: The Party and the Revolution. New York: Basil Blackwell, 1988.

Ruchwarger, Gary. People in Power. South Hadley, Mass.: Bergin and Garvey, 1987.

Rudolph, James D., ed. Nicaragua. Foreign Area Studies. Washington, D.C.: The American University, 1981.

Paraguay

Lewis, Paul H. Paraguay Under Stroessner. Chapel Hill: University of North Carolina Press, 1980.

Peru

Degregori, Carlos Iván. *Situación de Sendero Luminoso y de la estrategia subversiva después de la captura de Abimael Guzmán.* Lima, Peru: Instituto de Estudios Peruanos, 1993.

McCormick, Gordon H. *From the Sierras to the Cities: The Urban Campaign of the Shining Path.* Santa Monica, Calif.: Rand, 1992.

Strong, Simon. *Shining Path: Terror and Revolution in Peru.* New York: Times Books, 1992.

Uruguay

Gilio, María Esther. Translated by Anne Edmondson. *The Tupamaro Guerrillas.* New York: Saturday Review Press, 1972.

Kaufman, Edy. *Uruguay in Transition.* New Brunswick, N.J.: Transaction Books, 1979.

Labrousse, Alain. *The Tupamaros: Urban Guerrillas in Uruguay.* Harmondsworth, Eng.: Penguin Books, 1973.

Porzecarski, Arturo C. *Uruguay's Tupamaros: The Urban Guerrillas.* Praeger Special Studies in International Politics and Government. New York: Praeger, 1973.

Wilson, Carlos. *The Tupamaros, the Unmentionables.* Boston: Branden Press, 1974.

Venezuela

Valsalice, Luigi. *La guerrilla castrista en Venezuela y sus protagonistas, 1962–1969.* Caracas, Ven.: Ediciones Centauro, 1979.

MAGAZINE AND NEWSPAPER ARTICLES

General

"Terrorist Groups Battle Obscurity," by Rodolfo Windhausen, *Times of the Americas,* August 21, 1991, p. 10.

Bolivia

"The Last Days of Che Guevara," by David Reed, *Reader's Digest* 92, April 1968, pp. 74–80.

"Unwitting Betrayal," *Time* 90, November 24, 1967, pp. 33–34.

"What 100 Castro-type Guerrillas Can Do," *U.S. News and World Report* 62, June 26, 1967, pp. 84–85.

Brazil

"Death of a Guerrilla," *The Economist* 240, September 25, 1971, p. 45.

"Gunmen Kidnap U.S. Envoy in Brazil," *New York Times*, September 5, 1969, p. 1.

"How One Pleasant, Scholarly Young Man from Brazil Became a Kidnapping, Gun-Toting, Bombing Revolutionary," by Sanche de Gramont, *The New York Times Magazine*, November 15, 1970, pp. 43–45.

Chile

"Chile's Che Guevara? Miristas' Comandante Pepe or J. G. Lliendo," *National Review* 23, March 23, 1971, pp. 307–308.

"Pepe Captured (José Gregorio Lliendo)," *The Economist* 249, October 6, 1973, pp. 42–43.

Colombia

"Colombia's Guerrillas Break into Politics," by James Brooke, *New York Times*, June 3, 1990, IV, 5.

"Las FARC ¿El tercer cartel?" *Semana* (Bogotá, Colombia), February 14–20, 1988, pp. 22–27.

"El general en su laberinto," *Semana*, November 29–December 5, 1988, pp. 26–33.

"El gran negocio de la guerrilla," *Semana*, July 7–14, 1992, pp. 26–32.

"Guerra para rato," *Semana*, June 2–9, 1992, pp. 30–35.

"Guerrilla Group Surrenders Arms in Pact with Colombian Government," by Douglas Farah, *Washington Post*, March 3, 1991, p. A-18.

"Guerrillas Put Down Guns, Pick Up Want Ads," by Ken Dermota, *Times of the Americas*, August 21, 1991, p. 10.

"El petro-terrorismo del ELN," *Semana*, March 1–7, 1988, pp. 28–33.

"La república oriental de la guerrilla," *Semana*, June 2–9, 1992, pp. 36–37.

Costa Rica

"Decretan penas de 3 a 15 años para miembros de 'La Familia,'" *La Nación*, September 3, 1983, p. 6-A.

"En la mira del terror libio," *La Nación*, June 15, 1990, p. 5-A.

"Espionaje policial descubrió a grupo," *La Nación*, June 16, 1990, p. 5-A.

"Lento e incierto proceso por acciones terroristas," *La Nación*, April 5, 1982, p. 1-B.

"Procesados 15 ticos ligados con 17 delitos," *La Nación*, March 13, 1990, p. 10-A.

Dominican Republic

"Dead Rebels in the Hills," *Time* 83, January 3, 1964, p. 32.

Honduras

"Hostages Released from Honduran Jet," *New York Times*, March 28, 1981, p. 4.

Mexico

"Guerrillas Score," *The Economist* 247, May 12, 1973, pp. 45–46.
"Mexican Guerrilla Group Lashes Out at Leftist Newspaper," The Reuters Library Report, Reuters News Service, April 12, 1990, BC Cycle.

Peru

"Down the Shining Path," by Alma Guillermoprieto, *The New Yorker*, February 8, 1993, pp. 64–75.
"Rebel Leaders Admit Tupac Amaru Group Virtually Defeated," by Lynn F. Monahan, Associated Press, July 12, 1993.
"Sin Abimael, Sendero Luminoso es presa del descontrol ideológico," by Dominique Dhombres, *Excelsior* (translation from *Le Monde*), July 12, 1993, p. 1.

Uruguay

"Yesterday's Rebels Are Today's Politicians," by Jorge Baāles, *Times of the Americas*, August 21, 1991, p. 11.

Venezuela

"Bravo and His Boys: Venezuela's Castro-Inspired Armed Forces of National Liberation," by Milan Kubic, *Newsweek* 66, July 5, 1965, p. 47.
"Spreading Flames," *Newsweek* 59, June 18, 1962, p. 49.

About the Book and Author

Drawing upon primary as well as secondary documents, Liza Gross, with the assistance of the Council on Hemispheric Affairs researchers, systematizes the currently available information on revolutionary groups in Latin America and the Caribbean in one concise, accessible reference volume. The entries are organized by country, with each nation's guerrilla groups presented in alphabetical order. The author offers a multitude of vital statistics for each organization, including the year the insurgency coalesced, its principal leadership, and its core ideology. Each account provides the historical and political context for understanding how and why the movement emerged, reviews the organization's activities in detail, and explains its dissolution or present status.

This handbook will be an invaluable resource for students, researchers, academics, journalists, governmental and nongovernmental organizations, military analysts, and general readers with an interest in Latin America.

A native of Argentina, **Liza Gross** is a journalist and former executive editor of the defunct *Times of the Americas*. She has written extensively about Latin America for U.S. and Latin American publications and holds a master's degree in public affairs reporting from Ohio State University.

Founded in 1975, the Washington-based **Council on Hemispheric Affairs** has been described by Senator Edward Kennedy as "one of our nation's most respected bodies of scholars and policy makers."